To every individual who invested in my path. Nathan, Kirin, and Finnley, thank you for believing in me and cheering me on along the way!

contents

introduction

As a licensed clinical social worker, school mental health administrator, and former psychiatric social worker dedicated to working in schools and education for over 14 years, I have a different take on anxiety from the average person: I believe anxiety can be your superpower if focused with precision. Read that sentiment again: Anxiety can be your superpower if focused with precision. Think about it: Anything that challenges our brains to work hard and use emotions that are difficult to process while helping us develop psychological foundations that overcome our inherent freeze, flight, or fight instinct has the potential to promote a superpower level of existence.

This book is designed to teach tangible strategies that you can use to navigate social situations, overcome anxiety-provoking triggers, and individualize a plan to help you thrive. Life has bumps around every corner, but with the strategies put forth in this book, you will build a foundation to effectively mitigate social anxiety.

How to Use This Workbook

Social anxiety is a challenge that manifests in multiple facets of our daily lives. You may identify one area that is currently impacting you the most, such as asking questions in class or talking to new acquaintances. As you will see, social anxiety is like a leaky pipe: It can have a small effect almost immediately, but if it is ignored, it can burst and overflow into other areas of your life. To address this, this workbook is structured to tackle different aspects of your life, not necessarily just the identified problem areas. Using this book in its entirety will support those facets that you may not have identified as a struggle, and it will also help you manage triggers that you were not previously aware existed. The key to managing your social anxiety is arming your brain with strategic, sustainable tools.

Note to Parents and Caregivers

Social anxiety is an emotion that we all experience, and the level of its intensity is unique to each person. The first step is awareness. Awareness is not always easy and takes acceptance and reflection. As a parent it can be painful to see your child struggle with the stress of social anxiety, and you may have experienced emotions related to helplessness, frustration, and parental guilt. Sometimes we need a reminder that it is not a parent's role to shield a child from difficult emotions; rather, it is to be supportive and to assist your child in learning the skills and strategies needed to manage their anxiety rather than to avoid experiencing the emotions.

Understanding how social anxiety affects your child every day at home, school, and in other encounters is the second step in stress reduction and management. Learning positive coping strategies will provide lifelong tools to reduce stress and lessen the likelihood of maladaptive coping later in life. To help with this, you will find that this workbook incorporates a variety of practical exercises, each lasting approximately 10 to 15 minutes. As a parent, I want to emotionally equip my children to handle the adaptive demands of life, and I am sure that is why you have consulted this book. It is important to note that, depending on the level of social anxiety that is manifesting in your child's life, support needs to match that level of intensity.

CHAPTER 1

UNDERSTANDING SOCIAL ANXIETY

Welcome to the first step in understanding social anxiety. In this chapter you will learn its clinical definition and symptomology, which will help you distinguish between generalized anxiety and social anxiety. You will develop an awareness of how social anxiety impacts your life by taking a quiz and reflecting on the results. Through self-reflection you will learn how we instinctively use avoidance patterns to protect our brains when things are uncomfortable.

What Is Social Anxiety?

Social awareness is being aware of our actions and reactions when interacting with people in social situations. Social anxiety has the power to weaponize social awareness against you and your relationships when you fear being rejected or offending someone because of your behavior, and you constantly worry about how you are perceived by others. That fear of being judged, analyzed, or evaluated is magnified out of proportion to the reality of actual risk; essentially, this means the threat you perceive is not as dangerous as your brain is making the situation seem. Often this makes you feel small and can cause you to shrink in social situations.

Basic definition

Social anxiety is a mental health condition where one feels intense anxiety related to social interactions or performance settings. Unlike everyday nervousness, where you are nervous about a project or doing something new, social anxiety disrupts your life by causing you to avoid doing activities in social situations. Consequently, people with social anxiety can miss out on experiences or work opportunities that would positively benefit their lives.

Social anxiety vs. general anxiety

What is the difference between social anxiety and general anxiety?

Social anxiety is anxiety that is solely focused on a social situation where one must perform, interact, or be assessed by others in that specific situation. General anxiety is worrying about nearly everything, not just social situations. Common worries may include: *Will my parents ask about my homework? Will they ask about the test from last week? Am I wearing the right clothes? Is there a test today? Will my friends be in the same place at lunch?* Generalized anxiety disorder is characterized by having excessive worry more days than not, for at least six months. It is difficult for someone with generalized anxiety to control their worry thoughts. Those worry thoughts can lead to physical symptoms that affect how well a person can function, impacting their daily life. We call these somatic symptoms: physical symptoms that are manifested because of a mental state. It is important to acknowledge that these physical symptoms can cause a person high levels of stress that impair areas of functioning.

Let's look at the physical symptoms of general anxiety and how they negatively impact life:

- Feeling on edge and restless

- Having difficulty concentrating or focusing

- Irritability, where small things irritate you throughout the day

- Sleep disturbance (experiencing difficulty falling asleep, problems staying asleep, or restless or tossing-and-turning sleep)

- Muscle tension (having a tight or upset stomach, tight shoulders, or a tight or tense jaw)

- May experience trembling, unsteadiness, fidgetiness, or aches and pains

Symptoms of Social Anxiety

How does social anxiety show up day-to-day? When working on a group project you worry about how you greeted the group, and their criticism of your ideas or contributions becomes heightened. Before you go to your local coffee shop, you focus on the interaction before it happens. You think of all the things that can go wrong; you review your order like you are preparing to give a speech. (*Almond milk latte, hot, medium. Almond milk latte, hot, medium.*) You become narrowly focused on each word that leaves your mouth and evaluate the barista's reactions with a microscope. (*Did he smile at me? She was annoyed because I never said "hot." I was too indecisive between hot and cold.*) You may also review what you said after you leave. (*Please, medium almond milk latte. I should have said "please" last. Almond milk latte, please.*) Your words soon become a loop of judgment and self-loathing, which can quickly leave your self-esteem and self-worth in the gutter.

Symptoms of social anxiety include:

- Blushing or feeling the face become warm

- Shortness of breath

- Sweating, trembling, or having a shaky voice (stuttering, saying "um" a lot, or having a low tone)

- Tightness in the chest or a fast heartbeat

- Feeling lightheaded, dizzy, or faint

- Butterflies in the stomach, nausea, or an upset stomach

EXERCISE: SOCIAL ANXIETY SYMPTOM CHECKLIST

Read the statements below and check the boxes by statements you identify with:

☑ Social situations cause physical or emotional panic to set in.

☑ Avoidance is a key tactic in social situations due to my uncomfortable feelings.

☐ I worry excessively about what others think of me because of my actions or behaviors.

☑ I worry about feeling humiliated or embarrassed in social situations.

☑ I worry about sweating, stuttering, trembling, or blushing in front of people.

☐ I like to be in the background and never the forefront.

☑ I defer to family in social situations.

☐ I avoid direct communication.

☑ I obsess about my interactions with others.

☐ Often, I fortune-tell all the negative things that can go wrong.

☑ I feel isolated and gloomy.

☑ My mistakes echo and I focus on all the things I could have done better.

☐ "If" becomes a game I play in my head.

☐ I obsess on things and have obsessive tendencies like washing my hands multiple times.

☑ Perfectionism hinders me from moving forward, and I get stuck.

☑ I would rather use technology than interact with a person.

☑ People would refer to me as shy, quiet, or reserved.

☐ The thought of being the center of attention makes me cringe.

☑ I use technology overtly to avoid personal interactions.

☑ It is hard to build new relationships.

☑ To avoid socialization, I spend a significant amount of time with technology.

☑ When I feel that I do not know what to say or how to say it, I say nothing.

☑ Being close to someone physically or emotionally is very stressful.

Take the Quiz

Below are ten frequency statements that can help build awareness on how social anxiety may be impacting your life. Listen to your instincts when answering, as they will help you be honest with your answers. The goal of this activity is not to judge yourself; it is an opportunity for reflection and personal growth.

SCENARIO OR SITUATION	ALWAYS	OFTEN	SOMETIMES	RARELY	NEVER
In social situations, I fear I will embarrass or humiliate myself because of what I might say or do.	☑	☑	☐	☐	☐
I have feelings of discomfort in most social situations.	☑	☐	☐	☐	☐

SCENARIO OR SITUATION	ALWAYS	OFTEN	SOMETIMES	RARELY	NEVER
I worry about what I am going to say days before an activity (party, project, social situation).	☐	☑	☐	☐	☐
Daily interactions in my life (home, school, community, and relationships) are affected by my anxiety.	☑	☐	☐	☐	☐
I am tremendously aware of my actions and fear offending someone or being rejected.	☑	☐	☐	☐	☐
I prefer to be in the background in a group situation and not the center of attention.	☐	☐	☑	☐	☐
I avoid social situations and use technology as much as possible, so I do not have to interact with people.	☑	☐	☐	☐	☐
I am self-conscious that I will blush, sweat, or have a trembling voice when in social situations.	☑	☐	☐	☐	☐
Surviving social situations can be exhausting.	☐	☑	☐	☐	☐
I leave a social situation questioning my actions and obsessing over the things I said or what my physical actions were.	☐	☑	☐	☐	☐

Identifying your level of anxiety is important so that you can develop a strategy to manage your symptoms and reactions. Think of tackling this workbook like a ninja, with savvy and stealth, by obtaining skills and resources to reduce social anxiety. Together, we can move those quiz answers to the columns "Sometimes," "Rarely," and "Never."

How Is Social Anxiety Affecting You?

Let's dive in a bit deeper and examine how social anxiety has prevented you from engaging in various life-enriching opportunities. You may miss out at school by not making new friends or sustaining relationships because of the story that you created in your head about what others think or feel about you. Unfortunately, your perception skews your view of the world and ultimately bleeds into your future, filling you with doubt and insecurity.

One critical aspect is avoidance: We protect ourselves from intimidating situations by avoiding them. Think back to your own avoidance. What opportunities, actions, or encounters do you wish you had taken a risk with? It may have been trying out for a team or club, or volunteering in class, or answering a question to which you knew the answer. It can be small things that most people take for granted that impact your life most deeply. When we avoid these things, shying away from difficult feelings and declining opportunities, it becomes easier to take the road more frequently traveled.

Where is it showing up?

Social anxiety may leak into many aspects of your life and prevent you from achieving goals or otherwise hold you back, and your relationships may suffer. Together we can evaluate three areas that typically affect all of our lives: family, personal, and school/work.

Family. Family gatherings can overwhelm you with their associated expectations. One strategy you may have used is to fade into the background like a gnome in a garden. We know the gnome is there, but we focus on the brightly colored flowers and trees first.

Personal. You might have wanted to befriend someone or speak up in a group, but the anxiety in your stomach threatened your success and you were afraid of vomiting in public. Eating with people could also cause anxiety that you would personally like to avoid.

School/Work. Anxiety at school or work can cause your worrying brain to override your logic and intelligence. For instance, when you are called on in class or your boss seeks an answer to something you know and your words and thoughts are blank, you walk away with a prizewinning answer that no one had the chance to hear.

How do you respond?

In social situations, we are often self-conscious about how people perceive us; this can increase anxiety and create thoughts that are not based in fact. Self-consciousness can be like quicksand and it may feel like escape is not possible as each thought fires in your brain. Knowing what you are comfortable and uncomfortable with is the first step; you can use strategies from this workbook to combat your uncomfortable feelings.

Triggers are events or situations that cause uncomfortable emotions or psychiatric symptoms such as anxiety, panic, or unhelpful self-talk. Triggers can vary for each person, and may include one or more of the following:

- Talking in a group
- Working on group projects
- Public speaking or delivering presentations
- Being the center of attention
- Being introduced to someone new
- Ordering at restaurants
- Performing
- Going to parties
- Talking in line
- Meeting new people

- Family gatherings

- Family celebrations

- Being called upon for an answer

- Reading out loud in front of people

- Calling or talking on the phone

- Taking quizzes, tests, or essay exams

- Speaking to people in authority, like a boss or teacher

- Using public bathrooms

Once you know you are going to be in one of these situations, you can sidestep your anxiety by developing awareness, boundaries, and a plan. You can develop healthy boundaries by letting others know what you are and are not comfortable with.

Avoidance, escape, and safety-seeking behaviors

Our brains protect us by using defense mechanisms such as avoidance, escape, or other safety-seeking behaviors.

Avoidance. This involves any inaction or action a person takes to escape from difficult feelings or emotions. Think about delivering a presentation in school or at work: You avoid the action of delivering your presentation by calling in sick or hiding in the bathroom.

Escape. This occurs when someone takes a mental break from a stressful situation, either through daydreaming or dissociation, which is how people separate themselves from their current reality.

Safety-seeking behaviors. These are things we do that make us feel temporarily safe. They can be small things like avoiding eye contact, asking someone questions so the focus will never be on us, or wearing clothes (such as a hoodie) that hide physical reactions.

Avoidance starts a cycle that antagonizes anxiety, kind of like poking a bear; eventually, that bear will maul you. The anxiety that was the size of a Ping-Pong ball in your stomach slowly grows each day until it feels like you have a volleyball in your belly. That anxiety prevents you from being the best version of yourself because you limit your exposure to uncomfortable activities, which are key to personal growth.

ANXIETY AND YOUR BRAIN

Our brains are hardwired to avoid anything threatening and are equipped to instinctively protect us. Your brain is like a castle: Imagine the various defense mechanisms that a castle might employ, like a moat, a bridge, and even an alligator or two. In your brain-castle, the thalamus, or scout, controls your sights, sounds, and processes—what you see by size, shape, and surrounding cues. These are your castle's soldiers who stand guard over the terrain. They send signals to the cortex, or commander, which surrounds your brain-castle, providing meaning to these images. The amygdala (king or queen) is the emotional core of your brain and determines emotional significance. The locus coeruleus receives the call from the amygdala in times of need. The hippocampus is aware of anxiety and holds the baggage of your memories like artillery, ready to fire and connect memories to the emotion of the amygdala. All of your senses send signals like a communication system to the amygdala.

The hypothalamus and pituitary gland cause the adrenal gland, or the moat, to produce cortisol, a stress chemical in the brain. Too much cortisol makes it difficult for you to process a stressful experience and you lose perspective—your moat overflows. Your castle pulls up the drawbridge, as there is danger around you. Your soldiers go to work; the heart beats fast, you begin to sweat, and adrenaline floods your muscles. This is when your castle knows it is under attack. The freeze, flight, and fight instinct—your alligators—begins to take over, which can be very useful in a threatening situation. After all these responses are initiated, your consciousness becomes aware of the threat and evaluates whether or not it is real. The thalamus (scout) takes the information to the cortex (commander) to evaluate the level of threat. That sensory information will help your cortex determine whether to continue its fear response. Often the threat is caused by something triggered by a memory. For example, as a toddler you were told the stove is hot. At some point you challenged what you were told and touched the stove. You remember that the stove is hot, and so are rightfully afraid to touch it again.

When you experience social anxiety you perceive it as a real threat, which often makes it difficult to process information when your castle feels under attack. You have the power to train your brain to restructure how you perceive anxiety triggers. The path to symptom management is controlling your anxiety-triggered responses. This is where your castle can raise its flag in victory!

Avoidance: How to Identify and Avoid the Trap

A problem arises when your anxious mind perceives threats when, in fact, none exist. You use avoidance as protection to shield you from the false reality developed by your anxious mind. Avoidance is a temporary solution and is like putting a Band-Aid on a deep cut. It works for a minute until you realize you may need stitches or at least a few more Band-Aids. Avoidance becomes a warm shelter that defends you from anxiety for a fleeting moment, but at the cost of missed opportunities. How many doors have closed because avoidance was your protection?

Alternatives to Avoidance

Break the habit of shielding yourself through avoidance, escape, or safety-seeking behaviors by identifying your alternative options. Identify your safety-seeking behaviors ahead of difficult times and acknowledge that these behaviors do not reduce anxiety in the long run. Set boundaries and plan for the moments that you know set off the anxiety alarm by identifying what limits you need to set and what you are willing to endure. When I am at a family gathering, I have a few ideas ready so I can drive the conversation in the direction of topics I am willing to discuss. In these moments, being vulnerable and having anxiety may be too much; I share what I am willing to share. For example, "How are my grades? My grades are improving, and I am trying to organize my time to support both my assignments and my sports schedule. It has been a real challenge to balance between the two, and I am working on it." At a family gathering, what can you plan for? Think of where you will sit: You may want to sit next to someone who will not pepper you with questions, or someone who eats quickly. Plan for the things you can control.

ALTERNATIVES TO AVOIDANCE EXERCISE: IDENTIFYING ALTERNATIVE BEHAVIORS

Time: 10 minutes

An alternative way to cope is to seek help. Consulting with someone who has been through a similar situation may be helpful. I like to role-play a conversation that I know may be awkward or difficult with someone I know, such as a teacher, coach, boss, friend, or family member. I will ask them for feedback, practicing which words I should and should not use. Try asking someone in your life to help role-play a conversation that you need to practice.

Adjusting your expectations of a situation can be helpful when meeting new people. When I am introduced to someone new, my anxiety will rise because I worry that I won't remember their name. To combat this, I say their name in my head and try to associate it with someone or something I know my brain will remember. My expectation is that I won't immediately memorize someone's name, so I will have to make a special effort to remember. If you have a similar anxiety when meeting someone new, try using this simple trick and see if it helps!

Seeking help can be difficult if you don't want to expose your struggle. Vulnerability and openness may feel risky, but asking for help is a skill, and it shows strength. Practicing vulnerability can help us achieve great things when we open up and push ourselves to learn.

Practicing in front of a mirror is a great option when you are preparing for public speaking or an interview. You can see the emotions and thoughts, or nonverbals, that are transmitted by your face. The mirror provides an opportunity for reflection and practice. Try practicing in the mirror for ten minutes, or until you feel more comfortable.

Using a mirror may seem a bit silly. However, this is the easiest coping strategy because the only person in the room is you. You set the tone for embarrassment or laughter during your practice session. The risk is minimal, which makes this a great option. An added benefit is that you become aware of what others see. You may think, *When I am answering, my face is not as contorted as I thought*. Or, *I am smiling too much and I need to relax my face a bit*. The reward can be significant through awareness and empowerment.

Adjusting your expectations can be both easy and difficult. I have certain expectations for myself, and adjusting those expectations may be hard for me.

However, it can become easier if I understand that my expectations are unrealistic. For example, remembering the name of everyone I meet is not always achievable.

Where Do You Want to Make Change?

The changes and improvements we make to our lives usually reflect our values. Our values shape what we want out of life and the meaning that we attribute to aspects of our lives, like family, education and work, relationships, personal growth, and community. They essentially describe our purpose on the earth. Values guide our lives like a compass: They steer us in the direction that we are proud of, and they are the meaning of what matters to us. Our values can help us reframe our hardships and mistakes as areas for growth. I like to think of my values as a path toward the best version of myself. Being aware of our values can motivate us to do uncomfortable things and challenge ourselves to persevere. Taking advantage of our value compass reminds us of what is important and centers our intentions on the journey ahead.

EXERCISE: IDENTIFYING YOUR PERSONAL VALUES COMPASS

Time: 10 to 15 minutes

Psychologist Dr. Russ Harris created a list of common personal values, from which this list has been adapted.

Personal Values Assessment

Time: 5 minutes

Directions: Read the following list and mentally note the 10 values that are most important to you.

Acceptance: acknowledging and being receiving of myself and others

Adventure: seeking opportunities to create; exploring experiences

Assertiveness: speaking up honestly and respectfully

Authenticity: being my true self; staying original

Beauty: appreciating and growing beauty in myself, others, and my surroundings

Bravery: displaying physical or mental courage

Caring: showing kindness toward others and myself

° **Challenge:** pushing myself to develop, mature, and grow

Collaboration: being cooperative and working together

Compassion: having empathy for others' suffering without judgment

Connection: being present with others and connecting with what is in front of me

✓ **Contribution:** making a positive impact on humanity; adding to the world and helping it

Courage: being brave; facing my fears; persevering in times of difficulty or threat

• **Creativity:** being imaginative; developing new ideas; working outside the box and being innovative

Curiosity: having wonder; being eager to learn and interested in the unknown

Equality: following the Golden Rule and treating others as I would want to be treated

Excitement: being enthusiastic and pursuing activities that are inspiring

Fitness: enhancing my overall well-being, physically and mentally

Flexibility: being elastic; bending; adjusting to changing situations or environments

Freedom: having the power to act freely and live how I chose to live

Friendliness: being warm and approachable

Forgiveness: releasing resentment

Fun: seeking and engaging in enjoyable activities; creating fun; being fun loving

Generosity: being kind; giving and sharing

Gratitude: being thankful and appreciative of myself and others

Honesty: being heartfelt, sincere, and truthful

Humility: being unpretentious; staying humble; not boasting about accomplishments

Humor: finding comedy in life; appreciating and being aware of life's entertainment

Independence: being self-sufficient; leading my own charge

Integrity: being open and honest with strong ethical principles

Intimacy: being emotionally and physically available; having close personal relationships

Justice: standing up for equality; challenging oppressive behaviors

Kindness: having a loving disposition; showing consideration

Love: being warm, affectionate, and caring

Making a difference: having a positive effect

Mindfulness: being aware of my current experience and emotionally available in the present moment

Open-mindedness: looking at things with an open perspective; receptive to new ideas

Optimism: maintaining hopefulness and a positive view of the future

Patience: staying steady; accepting the time it takes for growth

Persistence: despite opposition, continuing to keep at it

Power: displaying leadership or influence

Respect: courteously appreciating myself and others

Responsibility: being accountable for my actions

Self-awareness: having personal awareness of myself and my thoughts, actions, and feelings

Self-care: taking care of my physical and emotional well-being

- **Self-control:** effectively regulating my emotions

- **Self-development:** identifying areas of personal growth for my character; skill building

Supportiveness: being compassionate and inspiring others

Trust: being sincere, genuine, and authentic

Vulnerability: being emotionally open; taking emotional risks

My Value Compass

Time: 3 minutes

Directions: Read the list of 50 personal values again. When you see one that stands out, write it on the list below to create a value compass.

Adventure
Authenticity
Challenge
Creativity
Humility
Independence
Making a difference
Open-mindedness
Self-awareness
Self-control
Self-development

Review the list you have created. The list can be viewed as a working list, and you can adjust it whenever you feel like one value becomes more important than another.

Awareness
Control
Development.

My Core Values

Time: 2 minutes

Directions: Review your My Value Compass list and star your top three. These will be your core values: the ones closest to how you define yourself.

Value Compass in Action

Time: 5 minutes

Directions: Write your top three values in the chart below by level of importance. Start with naming your value, and then noting why you picked that value. Next, describe what action it takes to live by that value. Consider how difficult it will be for you to complete the action. Finally, fill in how you will practice this value moving forward. An example has been included to help get you started!

VALUE	IMPORTANCE	ACTION	LEVEL OF DIFFICULTY	NEXT STEPS
Gratitude	I want to not take for granted the people and things in my life. I do not want to be ungrateful.	I need to acknowledge people when they positively contribute to my life.	Somewhat difficult	Practice gratitude by writing a list of five things I am grateful for each day.
Open-minded	I will only grow if I am willing to accept new things	I will listen to every contribution	difficult	I will not always make sure to fully consider everyones contribution before doing
~~Challenge~~ Adventure	I want to discover triggers and know as much as I can	I will always explore what I am told	Somewhat difficult	I will google search stuff I am told in class to find where it goes.
Make a difference	I want to be proud of myself and ~~accomplishments~~	I will use what I know to the best of my ability to make change	very difficult	I will plan the career path I think best suits me and execute & update the plan to give me the best chance of success.

Wrap-Up

As a result of chapter 1:

◆ We understand the symptoms of social anxiety.

◆ We have identified social anxiety triggers and built awareness of how anxiety impacts our lives.

◆ We have learned about the brain and how it functions like a castle to protect us.

◆ We have identified common triggers and how avoidance, escape, and safety-seeking behaviors are used as defense mechanisms.

◆ We have learned how to confront our anxiety and ways to not use avoidance, as it increases our anxiety by providing a false sense of reality.

FOCUS
ON THE
TASK
AT
HAND

FOCUS
ON THE
TASK
AT
HAND

FOCUS

CHAPTER 2

STRATEGIES THAT HELP

Mental health awareness has been around for thousands of years. Doctors, therapists, clinicians, and statisticians have described the problems and behaviors and their symptoms that impact our biological and social well-being. More than 70 years ago, the World Health Organization developed the term "mental hygiene." We typically use the word "hygiene" to describe how we care for our bodies by brushing our teeth, taking a shower, or washing our face. Mental hygiene describes what we do for our mental state: the activities and strategies that foster positive mental health, develop and sustain relationships, and help us make constructive changes in our lives. Numerous scientifically tested strategies are proven to reduce anxiety symptoms and break the cycle of avoidance. Just like how showering and brushing our teeth daily maintains physical hygiene, practicing good mental hygiene will improve our overall mental health and wellness.

Common mental health and wellness strategies include:

Mindfulness. Awareness of our thoughts and feelings, being present in the moment, and having awareness of our actions and the environment around us.

Acceptance. Being open to ourselves and acknowledging our feelings, both the difficult and the good. Acceptance encompasses our memories, beliefs, thoughts, ideas, goals, imaginations, and judgments.

Cognitive restructuring. The process in which we identify our distorted or inaccurate thoughts and challenge and reframe them.

Mindfulness

Being mindful will help you stay present and aware of your existing thoughts, behaviors, and attitudes; it is the baseline of where you are in the moment. Mindfulness is much easier to put into action when you are not feeling dysregulated and upset. Visualize a jigsaw puzzle box: it has hundreds of pieces jumbled together in one place. You open the box and all the pieces fall onto a table; it seems overwhelming to sort them all. But then you see a corner piece, and slowly you start to notice the pieces that will line the edges of the puzzle. When social anxiety is flooding your brain, sorting the puzzle pieces seems like a daunting task. Practicing mindfulness will help restore clarity to your brain when it overwhelms you with muddled, difficult emotions and distracting thoughts. Mindfulness has the power to help you untangle complicated thoughts and feelings by focusing your attention on the here and now.

With the many demands and distractions we face daily, mindfulness can be difficult. To minimize distractions, recognize what may break your focus. For example, I need to silence my phone and not have it in my line of sight. If it is on a table next to me, I put it away in my bag, which lowers the pressure I feel to be on top of email or messages in real time. However, it is also important to engage in mindfulness without pressuring yourself to have it look or feel a certain way.

MINDFULNESS EXERCISE: TODAY AND EVERY DAY

Time: 7 to 10 minutes

An intention gives you a purpose that can motivate and inspire; it is what you want to live by that day. It draws attention to the things you want to be more aware of by giving you purpose.

Step 1: Develop an intention.
Remember the three core values you listed? Take one and set an intention around it.

Step 2: Set your intention.
You should set your intention whenever you feel that you can make it realistically and consistently happen.

Step 3: Keep it visible.
You can write it on a paper or sticky note and put it somewhere where you will see it. You can also use your phone to take a picture of it, write it in your notes app, or set your phone's personal assistant to remind you throughout the day.

Step 4: Put it into action.
Find what will motivate you to put your intention into action. How will you notice the intention? Will you write it down, put it in a planner, or add it to your mental to-do list?

Step 5: Reflect.
It is important to reflect on the day and look back to see if you lived by your intention. If you were not as successful as you hoped, notice the barrier that got in your way. This is a learning opportunity and will help you prepare for success tomorrow.

Today and Every Day . . . Your Way

Step 1: Develop an intention.

I will be present in the moment and not worry about work that I have to do.

Step 2: Set your intention.

Focus purely on the task at hand and forget all other problems till I have dealt with the most pressing one.

Step 3: Keep it visible.

Screen saver

Step 4: Put it into action.

Step 5: Reflect.

Takeaway: When we learn how to do new things, rarely are we good at them the first time. Mindfulness is something to work on daily as part of our mental hygiene. It can be referred to as a "mindfulness practice."

MINDFULNESS EXERCISE: MY PERSONAL FORECAST

Time: 10 minutes

We check the weather to know what to wear for the day or week. Emotionally, we all have our own forecasts. With anxiety, it is important to be aware of that forecast and of how quickly a light wind can progress to a full hurricane. Getting ahead of the storm prevents us from experiencing negative feelings such as regret, embarrassment, stress, or anger.

1. List a moment that triggered your social anxiety:

_____

2. Make a list of five things that you were experiencing before the storm hit:

_____

_____

_____

_____

_____

3. Order the list of five from what affected you least to what affected you most.

_____

_____

_____

_____

_____

4. How did you reregulate yourself, or get yourself calm, in that moment?

_____

_____

_____

Takeaway: Mindfulness can also help you be aware of your thoughts and feelings and thus help you detangle them. Awareness is an essential component of making a change. You need to match your self-calming activity to the level of the storm. For instance, tell yourself a positive affirmation when you start to feel your stomach tighten: *I am safe, and this is uncomfortable, but doing uncomfortable things helps me grow.*

MINDFULNESS EXERCISE: ORDINARY KINDNESS COUNTS

Time: 5 to 10 minutes

It is hard to see the forest through the trees, so taking a step outside of our busy lives and focusing on other people helps us gain perspective. Doing something good for others helps us stay grounded.

Who: Think of someone who regularly contributes to your life in a positive way. Who "fills your bucket" and makes life better? Write their name here:

Dillon

What: Write how they add to your life:

They be a good friend Plays Overwatch with me

How: What is one simple thing you can do to add to their life? Write it here:

Plan: Decide on how you will achieve your act of kindness. Write it here:

Takeaway: Reflecting on how others fill your bucket brings a sense of gratitude. It allows you time to appreciate someone else and how they impact your life, even in the smallest aspects.

Exposure

In chapter 1 we learned that social anxiety prompts fear in social situations, and that fear is important and often keeps us safe because it is a warning that something is wrong. Through controlled exposure to fear, we create the opportunity to overcome those fears in a safe environment.

Exposure can happen in various ways:

In vivo exposure is being directly exposed to the object or situation in real life.

Imaginal exposure is imagining being exposed to the situation or object. A person will envision the fear, such as being in a dark room, in detail: what it feels like and what their thoughts are, exposing themselves to the fear through their imagination.

Virtual reality exposure is applied through technology, which is helpful when in vivo is not an option. Virtual reality can simulate experiences such as going on a ride at an amusement park or flying in an airplane.

Interoceptive exposure is purposefully bringing on the physical symptoms that are feared. Anxiety can make the heart race, so completing exercises that raise the heart rate like running in place, doing high-knees, or jumping rope are safe ways to experience the same feared physical symptoms.

We have all unintentionally used exposure to lessen our fears. As children, most of us were afraid of the dark, so without knowing it we practiced in vivo exposure—by going into a dark room, finding it to be safe, and then turning on the lights. Through repeating the experience over and over, we realized the result would be the same every time. (Unless a sibling or friend who thought they were funny jumped out and scared you!) The result was that 99.9 percent of the time—factoring in the sibling or friend—we were not harmed, which helped disprove the fear that the dark is a harmful place. Our brain rewired the dark room from being an uncomfortable place to being something we need not fear.

EXPOSURE EXERCISE: THE INTERVIEW

Time: 10 minutes

For most of us, being in an interview is anxiety provoking and can make us feel insecure. Think of what specifically triggers your anxiety in an interview.

Write down three to five of your triggers, in order of most anxiety-provoking to least.

1. _____

2. _____

3. _____

4. _____

5. _____

(Throughout this exposure, note your anxiety level on a scale of 1 to 10. The most extreme is 10: you are stressed to your limit. If you are at 1, you do not even flinch.)

Imagine yourself going to an interview. You walk through a door to an office and are instructed to sit in a chair covered in velvety gray fabric. What does the office look like? Is it cold or warm? Are the walls empty or decorated?

The interviewer sits down and begins to ask you questions. *"Tell me about yourself in two minutes."* Without escaping the room, you look down and feel the chair. It feels soft, and you take a breath and begin to answer the question. The interviewer says, *"Thank you. Please tell me your strengths and skills."* You see the wall behind the interviewer, and you focus on an object on the wall. Focusing on this object helps you answer the question. The interviewer replies, *"Thank you for your interview. We will let you know the result in a week or so."* You stand up holding a portfolio and walk out of the door you came in through.

Takeaway: Take a deep breath and high-five yourself!

EXPOSURE EXERCISE: IN VIVO EXPOSURE

Time: 10 to 15 minutes (each situation may vary)

It can be anxiety provoking and difficult to talk with someone in an authoritative position, such as a teacher, police officer, or supervisor. In this exercise, you will interact with someone of your choice in three steps, either on different days or over a period of hours.

Pick someone in authority with whom you regularly interact in a situation where you experience social anxiety, and write their name:

Step 1. Salutations (1 minute)

Salutations can be verbal or nonverbal methods of communication, such as greeting someone by saying hello or through a nod or wave. The goal is for you to initiate a salutation with your chosen authority figure. Write what your salutation will be:

Step 2. Question (4 minutes)

The goal is for you to ask a nonthreatening question (meaning in no way will the answer affect your relationship) to the person of authority.

Examples:

◆ "What is your favorite part of your job?"

◆ "What made you want to enter this profession?"

Write the question you have created:

Step 3. Disclosure

Disclosure is when you tell someone something that they did not previously know. It is at your discretion how personal you make this disclosure. Will it be at the surface level or will you go deeper?

Examples:

◆ "I find your class very interesting, and my favorite part is how you connect concepts to real life."

◆ "It seems overwhelming to learn all the things you need to know in your profession. I get intimidated when I think about all it takes to be a [fill in the blank]."

Write your disclosure:

_____

_____

_____

Takeaway: Pat yourself on the back and congratulate yourself for going outside your comfort zone!

EXPOSURE EXERCISE: INTEROCEPTIVE EXPOSURE

Time: 5 to 10 minutes

Get a chair or go somewhere where you can sit down and stand up easily. I recommend doing this exercise once while standing and once while sitting for the full effect; you choose which one to start with.

Step 1. Press your legs into each other and squeeze them together as hard as you can while counting to 10. (10 to 15 seconds)

Step 2. With your arms at your sides, bend them at the elbows. Each arm should be in an "L" position. Ball your hands into fists like you are holding something valuable in them and you don't want anyone to take it. Squeeze your arms together, engage your core by also squeezing it, and count to 10. (10 to 15 seconds)

Step 3. Tighten your face by forcing your eyes shut, squeezing your nose up, and making an angry fish face. Count to 10. (10 to 15 seconds)

Step 4. Combine all three together: legs, arms, stomach, and face at the same time. Count to 15 this time and really push yourself. Ready, 1, 2, 3: GO! (15 to 20 seconds)

Takeaway: You should have felt that same tense sensation that is uncomfortable when you have physical anxiety. By completing this exercise, you took that tense feeling (a somatic symptom) and re-created that feeling in a contained manner where you were in complete control.

Acceptance

Acceptance does not mean resignation. When it rains, we do not have the power to make the rain stop. We do, however, have the power to accept that it is raining and that we will probably get wet. How do we prepare for the rain? I personally wear rain boots and a waterproof jacket, and sometimes I will use an umbrella. We all make choices and decisions about how we choose to move forward. When it rains, we make decisions about clothing, acknowledge that water will touch our skin, and hope our shoes survive. Acceptance empowers us to take ownership of our feelings, our thoughts, and our actions.

Anxiety is part of life for 40 million Americans and 284 million people worldwide. Experiencing anxiety is a normal byproduct of life. The goal is to learn to manage the symptoms affecting us and to live a perfectly imperfect life, with anxiety being part of the path ahead.

ACCEPTANCE EXERCISE: YOU, YOURSELF

Time: 10 minutes

Sometimes, when we look in the mirror, we look for flaws instead of focusing on what is right about our appearance. But if you asked someone else what they saw, would they look for the flaws first or last? Our perceptions of ourselves can be like looking through glasses that are covered with fingerprint smudges. We can still see, sort of, but the view is skewed.

The goal of this exercise is for you to gain an objective view of yourself. Sometimes it is helpful to talk about yourself in the third person, so you can detach from your regular thoughts or opinions.

The following series of questions will help you look inward.

What would your best friend say are your top five qualities as a friend?

_____

_____

_____

_____

What are your favorite characteristics that you possess?

_____

What are the three key core personal values you live by?

_____

_____

_____

What is your superpower?

_____

_____

_____

Takeaway: *"If I've learned anything, it's that acceptance is the key to so much, and we find so much freedom in feeling fierce about what we're accepting."* — Jonathan Van Ness, *Queer Eye*

ACCEPTANCE EXERCISE: NO THANK YOU, THANK YOU

Time: 5 minutes

Think of an intrusive thought that comes into your head more than you would like.

How many times today did that thought show up and suck up your brain space and power? You may have tried to push it away and were unsuccessful.

Adopt the thought. Accepting it and being aware of its existence will take the power away from that thought and stop it from harassing you.

Try it for yourself.

Self-Compassion

Self-compassion is having empathy for ourselves when we make a mistake, come up short, or fail. Often, though, we shame ourselves in these moments of strife. Dr. Kristin Neff has researched self-compassion extensively and identifies three elements of it:

Self-kindness is being kind, being caring, and not criticizing ourselves.

Recognizing one's own humanity is acknowledging that we are imperfect, like everyone else on the planet.

Mindfulness is being aware of ourselves without judgment and staying present within our experiences.

We are frequently our own worst critics. There are several questions we can ask ourselves in difficult moments when shameful thoughts and feelings come up and we begin the slippery path of being self-critical and harsh.

◆ Would you say this out loud to a friend?

◆ What would you tell a friend in this moment?

◆ What would you tell your 10-year-old self?

Takeaway: Self-compassion is balancing acceptance of our imperfections and mistakes. It is caring for ourselves the way we would for a friend who was hurting. We turn that compassion inward and stop blaming ourselves for having flaws.

EXERCISE: SELF-COMPASSION

Self-Apology

Time: 10 minutes

We all need to give ourselves permission to have self-compassion. Think of a moment where you were your biggest critic. You shamed yourself and said mean, harsh things that you would not say out loud to someone else. Write a brief apology to yourself and then write one sentence thanking yourself for that mistake or error that you made, as it provided you with a learning opportunity.

_____

_____

_____

_____

_____

_____

_____

My Reflection

A second variation of the exercise is to use a mirror (or your phone's camera). Look at your reflection and do this exercise. Apologizing is a true skill and can surface difficult emotions; here is an opportunity for practice.

Repeat the exercise, using the mirror or recording it on your phone for playback and review.

Cognitive Restructuring

Our thoughts can get us stuck in quicksand where we slowly sink, but they also can motivate and inspire. Cognitive restructuring is the process in which we identify our distorted or inaccurate thoughts and reframe and challenge them. What is a distorted thought? Distorted thoughts are negative thoughts and beliefs that become a pattern in our brain, and we become convinced that they are true without any evidence.

Dr. David Burns has assembled a list of examples of distorted thoughts, which he refers to as "twisted thinking." These include:

All-or-nothing thinking. When you see things only as black and white; gray does not even exist. *I am either a rock star or a total failure.*

Overgeneralization. When you make a judgment about an experience or event and it becomes an ALWAYS or NEVER situation going forward. *I asked out a girl in my class and she said no. I am never going to get a date.*

Mental filters. You only focus on the negatives and filter out the positives. *You presented in class and your classmates and teacher told you positive things. Your teacher had one comment about what to improve the next time. You obsess over that one negative comment and replay it in your head on a loop.*

Discounting the positive. You discount or ignore positive experiences and belittle your accomplishments by dismissing them. *Your teacher or boss tells you that you did a great job and you dismiss it by thinking anyone could have done it. You got an A on a test and you think, "I just got lucky."*

Jumping to conclusions. You determine that things are negative without any supporting evidence. **Mindreading** and **fortune-telling** are also types of jumping to conclusions.

Mindreading: You make a negative assumption of what someone is thinking about you.

Fortune-telling: You make a prediction that negative things will happen.

Magnification or minimalization. Your perception is extremely skewed. This is called the "binocular trick" because you over- or underemphasize a situation. You blow things out of proportion and magnify the problem. *Because I did not get the promotion, I will never be promoted and now I am going to quit.* Or you shrink its importance. *The only reason I got the promotion was because no one else applied.* (I call this "making yourself small.")

Emotional reasoning. Your emotions become fact. You feel a certain way, therefore it is true. *I feel fat and that makes me fat regardless of my weight or body mass index.*

"Should" statements. You critique yourself or others with "should," "ought-to," "should not," "must," or "have-to" statements. It is important to note these statements bring out shame and guilt, which usually leads to anger and frustration. This is the self-deprecating talk we say about ourselves and others. *I should always be good at [insert your statement here].*

Labeling. You judge yourself or others and create a label based upon a mistake. *I did not say the correct answer in class. I am a total failure.*

Personalization and blame. You personally hold yourself responsible for something that was out of your control, or you blame others without taking responsibility for your contribution. *I got in that accident because I was running late this morning. The other members of my group did an awful job on that project and that is why I got a low grade (even though you did not help very much).*

By recognizing distorted thoughts, you have the power to restructure them. You can reframe, disprove, and change the pathways of your thoughts.

WHY, HELLO THERE . . .

Time: 15 minutes

Throughout this workbook, awareness, acceptance, and realization are essential concepts for you to use in order to progress. This exercise will help you put all three concepts into practice. Using the distorted thought patterns you just learned, identify which one you use.

Example:

Distorted Thought: <u>Minimization</u>

How do you use this distorted thought pattern?

I never give myself credit for what I do well. I dismiss when people compliment me because I think they are being fake or just saying nice things because they have to. It is hard for me to celebrate the things I am good at because it makes me uncomfortable.

How does this distorted thought hold you back?

I make myself feel small and then I have lower self-esteem. I think I am not good enough and feel like I am not worthy of success. Also, I do not push myself out of my comfort zone because I think I am not smart enough to do those things.

WHY, HELLO THERE . . . IT'S YOUR TURN!

Distorted Thought:

How do you use this distorted thought pattern?

_____

_____

_____

How does this distorted thought hold you back?

_____

_____

_____

Takeaway: We ALL have distorted thoughts and minimize ourselves with one thing or another. When we can see the destructive thought patterns, we can change the path! These thought patterns are time sinks, take vital energy from our brain, and diminish our true awesome selves.

Next steps: Become aware, accept this is happening, and realize you are in control of the pathway. Now reroute the pathway.

COGNITIVE RESTRUCTURING EXERCISE: NEW VIEW, DO YOU

Time: 10 minutes

Reframing is a strategy that keeps us from going down a dark, sad hole. Think of it as our sunny pair of glasses, through which things shine and the world looks a little brighter. Reframing helps us think of a situation from a new perspective by creating a different approach to viewing a situation, relationship, or ourselves.

Review the following five statements that summarize what your "friend" is experiencing. Find the positive in each statement and develop a new perspective for your friend.

1. *My parents are always in my business; it is so annoying.*

_____

2. *I am not smart enough to go to college or graduate school.*

_____

3. *My friend never called back; she must be angry with me.*

_____

4. *I have so much to do, and I will never have enough time.*

_____

5. *Making decisions is too difficult; I never make the right one.*

_____

Takeaway: Reframing helps us challenge our self-defeating negative thoughts. Looking at our problems as opportunities for growth helps us embrace challenges and allows us to view the things we struggle with as opportunities for improvement.

LET'S GO DEEP

Time: 10 to 15 minutes

One method of truly understanding the core of what is bothering you is called the downward arrow technique, because its goal is to get deep into an underlying issue and how it impacts you. Below are a series of questions that will get to your core fear. For this exercise to be effective, you need to practice vulnerability and honesty. This can be draining, as we often protect ourselves by burying difficult feelings. I encourage you to push yourself and rise to the challenge!

Situation: You have been invited by a classmate to attend a party this coming weekend. You are feeling anxious thinking about what to wear, who will be there, and how you will have to talk to new people. (If you feel that this situation does not apply to you, substitute a scenario more relevant to your life.)

What do you expect will happen?

Everyone will know each other and i'll be left on may own

What would be so awful about that?

I would feel awkward and like im distracting them from having a good time.

What does that mean to you?

I would ~~want to to leave~~ feel out of place

What would people say about you?

Judge me for being awkward and quiet.

If people said these things, what is the most awful thing that they would say?

Why are you here?

Why would this be upsetting?

Because I want to be with people but I would feel like I'm in their way.

What is the worst thing that could happen?

I leave

What feelings and thoughts are coming up?

loneliness.

Takeaway: These feelings and thoughts can prevent us from functioning in life. Can you see the true issue holding you back? Look at your answers. Can you name a distorted thought pattern? Think about how that distortion is not true, and then challenge it with facts and disprove it.

Jumping to conclusions, should statements

THE BENEFITS OF MINDFULNESS

Mindfulness has numerous research-demonstrated benefits, ranging from increased overall well-being to improvements in physical and mental health.

Overall well-being. Studies have shown that mindfulness and meditation foster a higher level of compassion. In fact, studies found that compassion for others and oneself increased, which leads to feeling more positive overall and higher levels of self-esteem.

Physical health. Mindfulness has been shown to decrease levels of pain and reduce rates of heart attack and stroke. Professional and Olympic athletes who have used mindfulness to enhance their level of play include Michael Jordan, LeBron James, Michael Phelps, Misty May-Treanor, and Kerri Walsh Jennings. Mindfulness can help quiet the noise and center an athlete, allowing them to focus on a specific task such as a free throw or an Olympic volleyball serve. Celebrities such as Jerry Seinfeld, Bill Gates, Kendrick Lamar, Lilly Singh, and Jennifer Lopez all use mindfulness to ground themselves.

Mental health. Mindfulness improves our mental health by reducing anxiety symptoms and lowering stress levels. It helps us develop an awareness of our feelings, thoughts, and emotions. Numerous ways to practice mindfulness exist, and mindfulness can be custom-tailored, which is why it is a great strategy for each and every person. The goal is that when we are dysregulated, we relax ourselves enough in order to become aware of our thoughts, physical state, and actions. In doing so we are not judgmental of ourselves, but are observers of the current moment.

Let's Get to Work

Daily practice is a routine that you do each day to improve any number of aspects of your life. You can want to improve, but without a plan, improving is only wishful thinking. Set time within your week to complete the next four chapters of this book. Keeping a steady stride will yield the best results. I use both an online planner and a written planner. Each gives a different perspective on my life: The online calendar is a view of my day, and my written calendar provides a balcony view of my week and month. Physical exercise benefits our bodies, but our brains benefit from a workout, too. To feed this need, pick two to three days where you can schedule 10 minutes on your planner to make use of this workbook. Life happens: If you are too busy one day, look for the white space on another day. Push yourself emotionally and mentally to complete the exercises in each section. They will give you tools to help you to reduce the anxiety that is negatively impacting your life.

Takeaways

"A goal without a plan is just a wish."— *Anonymous*

- Strategies such as mindfulness, exposure, acceptance, self-compassion, and cognitive restructuring can reduce social anxiety.

- Mindfulness can untangle difficult, muddled emotions and distracting thoughts.

- Exposure can happen in these four ways: in vivo, imaginal, virtual reality, and interoceptive.

- Acceptance is embracing our imperfectly perfect selves.

- Distorted thoughts impact our mental health, and restructuring them will—with practice—lead to a positive outlook.

- Scheduling time to complete this workbook will lead to learning new practices and will be a commitment to yourself. You would not quit on your best friend, so don't quit on yourself.

CHAPTER 3

SOCIAL AND HOME LIFE

Our social lives typically include making plans, going out, attending parties, and dating. The goal of this chapter is to learn lifelong strategies that you can apply to many of these situations and others, such as tackling awkward conversations.

Consider the following example:

Michael had a hard time making plans with friends. If someone invited him, he would go reluctantly, and Michael never invited anyone first. Michael felt pressure, anxiety about being rejected, and fear of being turned down. Michael realized his avoidance behaviors hindered his relationships, and he wanted to make a change. He pushed himself to be honest and worked to lower his anxiety. Michael learned to get comfortable with being uncomfortable. To be the best version of himself, Michael did the opposite of giving in to what was easy.

Home Life

Home can be a haven as well as a pit of angst. The demands of home can overwhelm all of us. There are things to do and people to please. Maintaining relationships can be physically and emotionally draining. Balancing the expectations that come with familial relationships can have you feeling like a tightrope walker in the circus. Anxiety can be triggered when we do not understand expectations, or we feel the expectations are not attainable. If you're like me, you're probably not a fan of questions being thrown at you without a break. *How was school? What did you learn today? Did you do X? Did you see Y? Where is Z?*

First, it is important to understand the expectations related to home life. I call these expected contributions—what tasks or items I am expected to contribute at home and the time they will take. Map it out. Break out your phone or planner and divide those contributions throughout the week when your schedule permits. Share with your household how and when you will complete your contributions. This should lower anxiety for everyone involved, as there is a map to success.

Second, a helpful trick is to practice asset-based thinking instead of deficit-based thinking. Is the glass half full or half empty at home? The glass half full is asset-based thinking. It is when you see the positive and appreciate what you have. Deficit-based thinking, on the other hand, is focusing on what is missing. Focusing on what you have and being appreciative leads to gratitude.

HOME LIFE EXERCISE: NOT FOR GRANTED

Time: 10 minutes

Research shows that gratitude leads to higher levels of happiness and lower levels of anxiety. People who express gratitude feel happier and are more optimistic about their lives. They feel more connected in their relationships, and this in turn helps them express their feelings. Gratitude also leads to higher levels of motivation and fewer avoidance behaviors.

Often, we take for granted the people closest to us. This exercise focuses on the people in your home and how they contribute positively to your day and to your life.

List everyone in your household. Next to each name, write one thing about that person that you are grateful for, or how they add something positive to your life. Do this each day for a week.

MONDAY	Mum cooks my meals P
TUESDAY	Mum can talk to about personal stuff P can talk to about fun stuff
WEDNESDAY	Mum cooks everyday for me and P
THURSDAY	Mum
FRIDAY	
WEEKEND	

Notes

Reflection: At the end of the week, review the list. Reflect on how you noticed these moments or acts. Ask yourself a few questions, such as:

◆ *Did I pay attention to these moments before this exercise?*
◆ *Do I show them gratitude now for these things?*
◆ *Do I say thank you regularly?*

Note your takeaways for the week. Sometimes, we forget to say thank you, or we assume the person knows we are thankful. Show gratitude to those who occupy the most important places in your life.

Awkward Conversations

Count to four slowly while you envision someone looking back at you, waiting for a response. Research shows it takes about four seconds of awkward silence in conversation before anxiety drastically increases.

Awkward conversations can be layered with uncomfortable feelings and physical reactions. We can feel embarrassed and even bothered by topics like mental health, sex, body image, social media, drug use, romantic interests, dating, academics, sports, or public performing.

When these conversations surface, we can do a few things that can help reduce anxiety.

Anxiety-reducing guidelines:

Plan the conversation ahead of time. This will help you prepare your brain and give you the opportunity to think of what you want to say.

Acknowledge your feelings. *"This conversation is uncomfortable for me and my anxiety is increasing."*

Strategize location. Pick somewhere that you feel comfortable, and stand or sit where you have access to a door or opening so you do not feel locked in.

Stay present. Focus on what is being said and do not fortune-tell what the other person is going to say.

Close it. Make sure you end your awkward conversation with a closure statement. That way, the conversation is not open-ended and it will be clear that it is over.

AWKWARD CONVERSATIONS EXERCISE: STAY BRAVE

Time: 10 to 15 minutes

Awkward and hard conversations can prevent us from being our best selves. The following rules were developed by Brian Arao and Kristi Clemens and can guide your next awkward or hard conversation.

Brave rule 1: Be courteous with controversy.
I am sure you have heard "Let's agree to disagree." Which translates to "Let's both stop talking and listening." What if we changed that to "I am open to hearing you, but I may have a different perspective." We can learn from others when they have a different opinion or view.

Brave rule 2: Intentions do not equal the impact. Own the impact.
We have all said things that did not land well. This can happen even when your intention was not to be offensive. When you offend, it is important for you to own the impact that your words had on the person. We all make mistakes and say things that were not meant to be hurtful; when they are hurtful, apologize and own the impact.

Brave rule 3: Show respect always.
Respect is given in various ways. It is important to consider culture, race, ethnicity, gender, religious affiliation, age, sexual orientation, and other factors when giving respect. You can show respect by being kind, polite, and grateful.

Brave rule 4: Make mindful choices.
We all must make choices. If you know nothing nice is going to be said, choose quiet. If you know deep in your heart it is important to challenge someone, stay kind when you do.

Brave rule 5: Do not attack.
When I feel backed into a corner, my defense mechanism is to attack so I am not "eaten" first. In an awkward or hard conversation, there may be a perceived risk of being eaten. We need to avoid causing malicious harm by intentionally hurting (or attacking) the person through statements we know will sting. Note that words like "always," "never," and "all the time" usually hurt.

Which brave rule do you feel is the easiest for you in challenging moments?

_____

Which brave rule do you feel is the hardest for you in these moments?

_____

How will you use these rules to improve your conversations in the future?

_____

_____

_____

AWKWARD CONVERSATIONS EXERCISE:
GUIDELINES + RULES = SUCCESS

Time: 10 minutes

ANXIETY-REDUCING GUIDELINES:	BRAVE RULES:
Plan the conversation ahead of time.	There can be courtesy with controversy.
Acknowledge your feelings.	Intentions do not equal the impact; own the impact.
Choose the location.	Show respect always.
Stay present.	Make mindful choices.
Close it.	Do not attack.

Using anxiety-reducing guidelines and the brave rules, let's practice a difficult conversation.

PLAN:

1. Run through the opening section of the conversation without fortune-telling what will happen.
2. Acknowledge your level of comfort and do a personal forecast (page 26).
3. Find a location where you can talk while feeling safe and not confined.
4. To stay present, think of something you can look at to keep you in the moment, and when you start to zone out or go to the future, look at it to remind yourself to stay in the moment.
5. Decide how you want to close the conversation. Presenting a solution or something you want going forward is a great way to wrap up.

ME: I need to speak with you about something that is hard for me to talk about. Could we talk at the kitchen table?

PARENT: Yes—can you give me five minutes to finish what I am doing? Then I will be there.

ME: Yes, thank you. [I sit in the chair away from the wall, where I feel the space is open.]

PARENT: Okay, what do you want to talk about?

ME: As I said, this is hard for me to talk about and I am feeling anxious, so I need you to listen and let me talk. Then, you can respond. I need you to not interrupt me, because that makes me more anxious.

PARENT: Okay, I will try, and you may have to remind me. I get excited sometimes.

ME: I am having a hard time . . .

> **Takeaway:** The guidelines and rules are strategies you can use in any conversation or interaction. Avoiding awkward or hard conversations can build resentment and animosity in relationships because your needs are not being met. You might get frustrated and blame that person in your life. Instead, take ownership and communicate your needs. Believe you are worth the few seconds of discomfort.

Having Friends Over

When you invite people over, hosting can feel like a hassle; it's one more thing to worry about. Trying to anticipate your guest's needs is for people who work in hotels and restaurants. Release the anticipation and anxiety of being the perfect host. Perfect is not an attainable goal, so reset your expectation to something achievable. One easy way to get ahead of this feeling is to ask your friends ahead of time what they like to eat and drink. Another is to ensure that they are not allergic to anything in your home, either food- or pet-related. (Having a friend sneeze or cough incessantly can put you both in a panicked state!) Stay true to, and authentically be, your perfectly imperfect self.

HAVING FRIENDS OVER EXERCISE: STAY OUT OF THE BOX

Time: 10 minutes

Flexibility is the ability to change, compromise, or bend—all without breaking. We can set plans, but life often takes us for a detour. With these turns and bumps in the road, we need to learn to adapt. We need to adjust and compromise as things evolve. When a friend is visiting, flexibility helps when these turns happen naturally. For this exercise, being "in the box" means you are determined to stick to your original plan or usual pattern. Staying "out of the box" means that you find ways to adapt and be flexible.

Creativity helps us stay out of the box. Be creative in the moment. If you or your friend has a fun idea, it should be all right if you do not do what is planned. You may find a commonality in something that you were unaware of before. If your anxiety begins to increase, shift your focus.

Shift your focus when your thoughts start to get ahead of you. Think of what is going well and what things are making you have a good time. Focus on what you are enjoying by using your mindfulness skills and being present.

Hint: Using the cognitive restructuring skills from chapter 2 can be your secret weapon in these situations.

Write down examples of how you have stayed outside the box:

Ex: [The movie was sold out, we bought tickets to another movie and walked around with the leftover time.]

Reflection: In the list that you created, think of how you managed your anxiety. What do you need to do to keep your anxiety managed in order to stay out of the box with friends?

Example: I need to remember that controlling everything is not possible and shift my thoughts to be present.

HAVING FRIENDS OVER EXERCISE: COME ON OVER

Time: 10 minutes

Amy wants to invite two friends to her house this weekend. Kathy sits next to her in one of her classes. She smiles at Amy and they chat in class most days. The other friend, Samantha, is on Amy's team outside of school. They often joke and laugh at practice, but they have never spent time together outside of team events.

Tip: Talk about what activities you will do ahead of time. Having an idea of a few things or activities you can do will lower your anxiety and level of anticipation about what is next. This should help you stay present and enjoy the time with your friend, as opposed to worrying about the next thing, and the next thing.

Visualize how you would communicate if you were Amy. We all have our preferred method of communication: over the phone, through an app, via text, etc. Think about what you would actually use; that way you will feel the most comfortable.

AMY: Hey Kathy, it's Amy from class. What are you up to? Are you around today?

KATHY: I think so.

AMY: Do you want to come over and hang out?

KATHY: Sure.

AMY: How long can you hang out for?

KATHY: A few hours. I need to be home for dinner.

AMY: Okay. I was thinking about inviting one of my teammates, too—Samantha.

KATHY: Okay.

AMY: Do you want to [watch TV, listen to music, play video games, etc.]?

KATHY: Yes, that sounds fun.

AMY: Do you need a ride over?

KATHY: I can ask.

AMY: Okay, let me know.

Your turn! Now practice inviting Samantha as if you were Amy.

_____

_____

_____

_____

_____

_____

_____

_____

_____

_____

_____

_____

_____

_____

_____

_____

FAMILY MATTERS

Social anxiety can impact physical and emotional closeness in our familial relationships. A familial relationship can be any relationship with someone you consider family—those who live with you or who are culturally considered family. As we are establishing our personal identities, these relationships may make us feel self-conscious, judged, or analyzed. These people have the most value in our lives and we want them to be proud of us.

At family gatherings, being the center of attention can feel like an interrogation scene in a movie—spotlight above your head, sweating, and all. You may worry about your actions and behaviors when around family members. Just thinking about holiday gatherings may spark anxiety. Maybe you have a loud aunt or cousin who pokes fun at you, and that triggers your anxiety. Let's call them Cousin Alex.

The solution? Have a strategy (or five) depending on your level of anxiety. You cannot control everything, but you can show up prepared.

Strategy 1. Use the My Personal Forecast exercise (page 26) to monitor your anxiety level.

Strategy 2. Which supportive ally will be there at the gathering, holiday party, or family dinner? Let that person know that Cousin Alex triggers your anxiety. Your ally can support you, and letting someone know helps dissipate the burden.

Strategy 3. Brave boundaries: Keep your boundaries and stay brave. Take this opportunity to let Cousin Alex know that being peppered with questions is uncomfortable, or that getting asked in front of family who you are dating is beyond awkward. Give Cousin Alex the opportunity to see you and your boundaries.

How Is My Social Life?

Introspection is the examination of our mental and emotional processes. Through introspection, we have the opportunity for personal growth. Personal growth is the lifelong process of understanding, learning, assessing, and reflecting on areas of personal development. By examining our processes, assessing, and reflecting, we expose ourselves to our full potential.

The first assessment will help you evaluate how frequently social anxiety is impacting your life. A positive step forward is reflecting on when and how often anxiety is showing up. For you to take the next step, awareness is required. The second assessment will help you evaluate avoidance patterns and behaviors. Avoidance can feel in the moment like relief. It masks itself as a helpful tool when the reality is that avoidance is a friend to no one. Avoidance can foster anxiety like a small, seemingly inconsequential snowball that rolls down a hill, eventually creating an avalanche.

Assessments can sometimes spark anxiety. However, you will be the only one who knows and who will see the answers. Dr. Patrick Spencer Johnson said, "Integrity is telling myself the truth. And honesty is telling the truth to other people." Let's start with telling yourself the truth, and we can work on other people later.

SOCIAL LIFE ASSESSMENT: IMPACT

The following quick set of questions evaluate how often your social anxiety impacts your life. When answering, it is important to think of these questions about your feelings in terms of the last two weeks to one month. Check the box that most accurately describes how often you felt the statement during that time.

QUESTION	NOT AT ALL	SEVERAL DAYS (MORE THAN TWO DAYS A WEEK)	MOST DAYS	ALMOST EVERY DAY
When I walk into a room, it feels like all eyes are on me.	☐	☐	☐	☐
Speaking up for myself is uncomfortable.	☐	☐	☐	☐
Eating lunch with others is stressful.	☐	☐	☐	☐
I feel uncomfortable speaking in public.	☐	☐	☐	☐
I think about talking to people before it happens and practice the conversation in my head.	☐	☐	☐	☐
People say that I am shy or quiet when they describe my personality.	☐	☐	☐	☐
I struggle to express my opinion.	☐	☐	☐	☐
Being the center of attention is uncomfortable.	☐	☐	☐	☐
I do not like inviting people to do activities or go places.	☐	☐	☐	☐
I fortune-tell all the things that can go wrong.	☐	☐	☐	☐

Add up your scores:

Not at all: _____

Several days (more than two days a week): _____

Most days of the week: _____

Almost every day: _____

The higher your scores are in the three columns toward the right, the more frequently anxiety impacts your life. Awareness is the first step. I encourage you to keep pushing yourself and to be honest in the process. Honesty will always have better results; it will shape your integrity.

SOCIAL LIFE ASSESSMENT: MY AVOIDANCE PATTERNS

In chapter 1, we learned how avoidance patterns protect our brains when things are uncomfortable. Here is a quick set of questions to help you understand your avoidance behaviors.

Check the box that most accurately describes your response to each statement.

QUESTION	STRONGLY DISAGREE	DISAGREE	AGREE	STRONGLY AGREE
I avoid social situations.	☐	☐	☐	☐
I use technology to communicate as much as possible, such as ordering food online.	☐	☐	☐	☐
When I go out, I make sure someone is always with me.	☐	☐	☐	☐

QUESTION	STRONGLY DISAGREE	DISAGREE	AGREE	STRONGLY AGREE
To make myself feel less anxious, I wear my hair a certain way (for example, in my face) or wear certain clothes (for example, a hoodie).	☐	☐	☐	☐
I look at my phone so I do not have to talk with people in public (like while waiting in line or standing somewhere).	☐	☐	☐	☐
I self-soothe in social situations (for example, I bite my nails, rub my arm, or pick at something) to reduce my anxiety.	☐	☐	☐	☐
If I am invited to a group situation, I make up a reason why I cannot do that activity.	☐	☐	☐	☐
I avoid eye contact so I do not have to talk to people.	☐	☐	☐	☐
I do not like asking questions in public, like at a store or restaurant.	☐	☐	☐	☐
I do not like confrontation, so I do not add my opinion in most situations.	☐	☐	☐	☐

Add up your scores:

Strongly disagree: _____

Disagree: _____

Agree: _____

Strongly agree: _____

If your scores were mostly "agree" and "strongly agree," you are likely experiencing avoidance patterns. It would be beneficial to know what behaviors have become a habit to help you deal with the moment. We learned in chapter 2 that avoidance further increases our anxiety.

Social Media

In 2018, there were 243.6 million social network users in the United States, accounting for 21.4 percent of total mobile minutes used. According to that statistic, our lives are entrenched for a good portion of the day in social media. Social media allows us to engage, chat, message, post, respond, view, learn, get inspired, display creativity, scroll, read, connect, rinse, and repeat.

We must ask ourselves two questions about mental wellness on social media, thereby creating much-needed social media mindfulness:

- How do we balance the fact that it can never be turned off?

- What do we do when we are caught off guard and anxieties appear?

First, let's identify when social media increases our anxiety.

- We put pressure on ourselves to post positive and attractive things about ourselves. We use filters to enhance photos and show highlights from our lives.

- We were not invited to an event but we see people posting about it. We see friends doing something, going somewhere, and having fun, and we were not included.

- *How many comments and likes on posts will I get? When I post this, will it go viral?* Or, *This is not going to get many likes, so I shouldn't post?*

- We have no control over what someone posts about us, and we see it. Free speech has its benefits and costs. This can take an emotional toll we were not prepared to pay.

- Awareness is truth. By identifying what sparks our anxiety on social media, we can plan to manage the causes of anxiety.

SOCIAL MEDIA EXERCISE: MINDFULNESS

Time: 10 minutes

Relieving the pressure of social media is our first challenge. To do this, we need to create social media mindfulness.

List some ways in which social media impacts your thoughts or feelings negatively and positively:

POSITIVE THOUGHTS OR FEELINGS	NEGATIVE THOUGHTS OR FEELINGS

Review the list. There is always a cost/benefit ratio for me when I evaluate components of my life: what something is adding to my life—the benefits—versus what it is taking away from my life—the costs. Social media can both benefit and cost, so it is important to reflect on whether you are feeling more negative than positive effects.

If your thoughts and feelings are mostly negative reactions, you may need to take a break. Taking a break can help you be more mindful of the relationships, connections, and activities that you enjoy in your daily life. When you return, stay aware of the anxiety triggers that bring on negative thoughts and feelings. Focus on the positive things that social media provides, and make note of those moments. We can increase our positive feelings and emotions by repeating the activities that sparked those moments.

SOCIAL MEDIA EXERCISE: REAL LIFE VS. REEL LIFE

Time: 10 minutes

The pressure is *real* to live a *reel* life on social media. On social media we only show perfect highlight reels of photos and videos, share the funniest things, and so on. We want to post the best photo and show that we are amazing because we are in [insert exciting place here]. We use filters to brighten, change contrast, add texture and tone, and modify colors, all resulting in changes to our real appearances. Real life is different from reel life.

"What I've learned is that living in public life . . . it's impossible to have everybody like you. No matter what you do." —Antoni Porowski

"WHEN PEOPLE BUILD UP WALLS, THEY END UP KEEPING OTHER PEOPLE OUT. BUT THEY'RE ALSO KEEPING THEMSELVES IN."
—Karamo Brown

"You being your true self isn't going to offend anybody . . . if they're concerned, that's on them." —Tan France

"I was always told to stay between the lines, so I drew my own."
—Bobby Berk

"Don't forget to love yourself." —Jonathan Van Ness

Write five affirmations about your REAL life that you are proud of, that make you smile, that you own without apology, that make your real life worth living.

Example: I am hilarious even if I am the only one paying attention.

1. _____

2. _____

3. _____

4. _____

5. _____

"Focus on how to be social, not on how to do social."

—Jay Baer, founder of Convince & Convert

SOCIAL MEDIA EXERCISE: AVAILABLE ALL THE TIME

Time: 10 minutes

It is not realistic to be available 24/7. Setting boundaries is a healthy practice—too much of anything is not healthy. I love cookies, and eating one cookie is okay, but eating the box, not so much. Social media is the same. Limiting yourself and setting boundaries is healthy, so live your real life more than your reel life. Additionally, research indicates that nighttime social media use can reduce sleep quality and add to anxiety. It is recommended not to use screens two hours before bedtime to reduce blue light exposure; this tells our bodies to wind down.

Set a schedule: Healthy screen time means not using screens all the time. Make a commitment to shut it all down at a certain time at night to give yourself a break and get quality sleep.

See the following chart, broken into three times of day: morning, afternoon, and evening. You can also choose to break your day into smaller time slots. Small bites work better.

My social media schedule:

DAY	EXAMPLE	MON	TUE	WED	THU	FRI	SAT	SUN
Morning	Before I leave, 10 minutes.							
Afternoon	When I am not busy, 10 minutes or less.							
Evening	off by 9:00 p.m.							

DIGITAL CITIZENSHIP

Digital citizenship means using technology responsibly by following our personal values and observing social norms online. We practice digital citizenship by developing digital literacy, staying safe online, and understanding digital health and wellness.

Digital literacy is how we use information and technology to communicate, find, evaluate, and create. Before digital literacy existed, we told stories, asked a neighbor, or consulted books as our sources of information. Technology has provided an amazing resource of information that is absolutely helpful, but also potentially extremely hurtful. When wielded with responsibility, information is our most powerful tool.

Online safety is an essential part of being responsible online. It is easy to say things through a screen because the positive and negative consequences manifest differently than in person. Words have the power to hurt or inspire, and you choose how to use them. If you feel drained by reading someone's posts or are offended by them regularly, be mindful and disengage.

Google has developed a collection of Digital Wellbeing Experiment applications, which they define as "tools that help people find a better balance with technology." Examples of these include:

Paper Phone. You choose all the important things you need from your phone, and this app will print a paper version. You will have all the information you need for the day and can take a little break from your digital world.

We Flip. A group challenge to all stay off of your phones together.

Desert Island. You select the apps that you absolutely need in order to function, and you challenge yourself to use only those apps for a set period of time (for example, one day).

Making Plans with Friends

Joseph was funny and always laughing, but on the inside, he was full of disruptive thoughts and his social anxiety was thriving. Just like Michael from earlier in the chapter, he had a hard time asking friends to hang out. Joseph liked to blend in and could bounce from group to group. He feared being embarrassed by saying the wrong thing or looking anxious. Joseph worried that people would notice him sweating, so he always wore a jacket no matter how warm it was outside. Often, he would back out of plans or ignore an invitation as an avoidance tactic.

Joseph needed more assurance from his friends. Concrete plans lowered his anxiety, and planning helped him question things less. The strategies in this section will support you in knowing your value as a friend. You will have the opportunity to practice, which will increase your confidence. Last, you will obtain information on making decisions.

MAKING PLANS WITH FRIENDS EXERCISE: 20/20 VISION

Time 10 minutes

Here are 20 adjectives that might describe a friend and five blank boxes for you to add your own. Add adjectives to the five empty boxes before you go on to the next part.

Honest	Protective	Humorous	Patient	Accountable
Kind	Respectful	Transparent	Accepting	Nonjudgmental
Trustworthy	Fun	Supportive	Understanding	Dependable
Considerate	Forgiving	Selfless	Encouraging	Genuine

Circle or highlight the adjectives that describe the qualities you think make a good friend.

In the next chart, write ten adjectives your friends would use to describe you. **My friends would say I am . . .**

Reflection: A true friendship is a symbiotic relationship: Where one gives, the other also gives, and both benefit. If you do not value yourself as your friends do, the relationship is uneven. You are priceless. Know your value.

MAKING PLANS WITH FRIENDS EXERCISE: PRACTICE CREATES CONFIDENCE

Time: **10 minutes**

Here is an example of making plans; read the dialogue.

Asher wants to hang out with his friends over the weekend. At lunch he decides to make plans and see if his friends are interested.

ASHER: I want to see a movie this weekend. I haven't been to the movies in forever.

RYAN: Yeah, that sounds cool.

NATHAN: I'm around this weekend.

ASHER: What movie should we see?

RYAN: Let's look at what is playing. I really only like that one theater by your house.

NATHAN: We'd better get tickets before we go—that place is always busy.

ASHER: Here is a list of times and movies. I think Saturday night, because I have family plans.

RYAN: Yeah, I have breakfast on Sunday with my family, so either Saturday day or Sunday night.

NATHAN: I can do whatever—no plans this weekend.

ASHER: How about Saturday at noon—there's the new Marvel movie.

NATHAN: Yeah, that sounds good.

RYAN: I can do that, too.

ASHER: You want to meet at my house like at 11:30 a.m.?

RYAN: Sure.

NATHAN: Okay, cool.

Now practice creating your own conversation that you would have with your friends. By practicing asking and thinking of how to set plans, you will help your confidence stay strong in the moment in real life.

_____

_____

_____

_____

_____

_____

_____

_____

_____

MAKING PLANS WITH FRIENDS EXERCISE:
DECISIONS, DECISIONS

Time: 10 minutes

In chapter 2, we learned about how our brains make decisions and that when our anxiety is high, our decisions suffer. Our feelings tell our brains there is risk, and our thoughts can add to the situation when they are fueled by fear. Our actions tend to be directed by this chain of command:
Feelings → Thoughts → Actions.

When making plans, having certain information may help slow your anxiety from unleashing your alligators for protection. An avoidance behavior may try to kick in, such as acting indifferent and saying you do not care and that whatever is fine. Or you say yes, but you create an excuse to get you out of the plans: "I have a ton of stuff to do." Remember, the perceived risk is higher than the actual level of risk.

What information do you need to feel more secure in saying yes?

Who: Knowing who is going to be there may help reduce your anxiety.

What: Doing something physical may be a great idea, as there is less pressure to talk all the time. Also, being physical is a great way to get adrenaline out of your system.

Where: Certain places and activities are less intimidating, like going to the movies. Communicate your needs to your friends.

When: Time is an essential piece of the puzzle. Knowing how much time an activity should take will give structure.

Practice: Answer these questions before making plans to determine what you need for your brain to feel good.

Who: _____

What: _____

Where: _____

When: _____

Reflection: Remember, perceived risk is higher than the actual level of risk.

Going Out with Friends

When you're planning to go out with friends, your anxiety may disrupt your sleep, interrupt your focus, and make you feel irritable toward others. Your thoughts may criticize you before you even exit your house.

Kimberly loved going out with friends. However, once she was out, her anxiety seemed to take control and she felt more like a passenger along for the ride. Kimberly struggled with her emotional push and pull. She had fun with her friends and liked going out. Yet she also felt her anxiety weighting her down. The strategies you are about to learn—calm affirmations, deep breathing, and brain dumping—will help you manage anxiety symptoms when going out with friends.

GOING OUT WITH FRIENDS EXERCISE: CALM 1, 2, 3, CALM

Time: 5 to 10 minutes

Having a saying, affirmation, or mantra can give you a sense of control when your feelings would otherwise be spinning out of your reach. Every day you can use this word or phrase to gain a sense of control. "Calm 1, 2, 3, Calm" can be used in any situation.

Close your eyes and say *Calm*. As you breathe in, count *1, 2, 3*. As you breathe out, repeat *Calm, 1, 2, 3*.

Write your own mantra below that you will use when you feel your personal forecast begin to shift.

_____

_____

You can potentially restore your sense of control and return to baseline in ten seconds. Be aware of your personal forecast, and when you are starting to feel the storm, begin your mantra. Breathe in, *Calm, 1, 2, 3*, breathe out, *Calm, 1, 2, 3*. This exercise should help you reregulate and will return you to a peaceful forecast.

GOING OUT WITH FRIENDS EXERCISE: BRAIN DUMP

Time: 5 minutes

Brain dumping has a few meanings. One definition is that you take information and transfer it to another storage location. Another definition is that it's an act where you express your thoughts, feelings, and ideas without judging them. Together we are going to combine these definitions. Our thoughts can take up an extensive amount of cognitive energy and space. In fact, keeping them in your head can feel like a job that you do not get paid for! We often don't realize how much mental energy we are using daily on our thoughts.

For this exercise, you need a timer (phone, smart watch, etc.), paper, and a pen or your preferred electronic device. Set a timer for two minutes and write down as many worries, ideas, and feelings as you can think of about going out with your friends.

_____

_____

_____

_____

_____

_____

_____

_____

_____

_____

_____

If you felt like two minutes went too quickly, add another minute. The idea is to let go of your immediate thoughts and not dwell on them. Add small increments of time as necessary, but stay under five minutes.

Reflection: You should feel emotionally lighter and cognitively less heavy. You can use brain dumping in many situations. Stressed over how much work you have to do? Brain dump it. This can also help before exams. (Bonus! This workbook just snuck in a study tip.)

GOING OUT WITH FRIENDS EXERCISE: BREATHE THROUGH DISCOMFORT

Time: 5 minutes

Research shows that deep breathing, or diaphragmatic breathing, has significant health benefits. In fact, studies show that those who practice deep breathing have lower levels of cortisol, the stress chemical.

Additional health benefits include:

◆ Increases oxygen supply to the blood

◆ Calms the mind and body

- Reduces stress and anxiety

- Releases tension in the muscles

- Helps build mindfulness

- Promotes focus, making you feel smarter

You can practice deep breathing anywhere, at any time, which allows this exercise to travel wherever your anxiety travels—out with friends, on a date, at dinner with your favorite aunt and uncle, and so on.

There are many ways to practice deep breathing. This exercise will teach you a simple practice that you can perform undetected in front of anyone. You are going to breathe in and count to four. Then you are going to hold the air and count to four. Last, you will breathe out while counting to four. Do this by breathing in through either your nose or mouth, whichever is most comfortable (or least noticeable) for you.

- Ready? Let's try. *Breathe in 1, 2, 3, 4. Hold 1, 2, 3, 4. Breathe out 1, 2, 3, 4.*

- Again. *Breathe in 1, 2, 3, 4. Hold 1, 2, 3, 4. Breathe out 1, 2, 3, 4.*

- One more time. *Breathe in 1, 2, 3, 4. Hold 1, 2, 3, 4. Breathe out 1, 2, 3, 4.*

Research also shows that if you do this consistently twice a day for six weeks, you will see your heart health improve, which ultimately will help lower stress and anxiety. Win-win!

Going to Parties

Parties can have physical, emotional, and behavioral anxiety triggers. You may worry about all the things people are judging you on, and you may experience physical symptoms, such as your heart racing and your hands sweating. Behaviorally, you may cling to your best friend or the person you came with. Avoidance may be your warm blanket in situations that challenge your anxiety on all three levels. Stay focused. Avoidance prolongs your anxiety and often masks itself as a helper. Parties are a great way for you to challenge yourself by making a game plan, preparing successfully, and having a coping strategy.

GOING TO PARTIES EXERCISE: GAME ON

Time: 10 minutes

There are only two players in this game: you and yourself. One part of you will play the game and the other part will keep yourself accountable. Set small tasks to be completed, like you are completing a scavenger hunt. The scavenger hunt allows you to set small goals for yourself at the party.

Scavenger hunt ideas:

- Talk to five people.

- Introduce yourself to two people whom you do not know.

- Stay at the party for a set time (one hour, 90 minutes, etc.).

- Find three people who are wearing the color blue.

- Find a safe place at the party for your deep breathing.

- Use a specific word in conversation that is a challenge to incorporate, like a code word.

- Try one food item that you would not usually eat.

- Find the colors of the rainbow at the party (in the room, on clothes, etc.).

- Look for three objects that you also have in your house.

- Think of two things at the party that rhyme (such as floor and door).

Create your own list of three things to hunt for or do at a party:

1. _____

2. _____

3. _____

Setting small goals will keep you focused on moving forward. Also, it is a fun way to distract yourself from anxiety symptoms, like unhelpful thoughts or your annoying inner critic. At the end of the party, acknowledge the things you challenged yourself to do and give yourself a mental high-five.

GOING TO PARTIES EXERCISE: LIGHT BULB

Time: 10 minutes

Preparation can set your fortune to success. What do you need in order to shine at a party? Let's take our three categories of symptoms and prepare them for positive results.

Preparation List:

Physically:

◆ Pick out your clothes ahead of time, and wear something comfortable that you feel good in. You do not want to be fussing with something itchy or tight, making yourself even more self-conscious.

◆ Refrain from things that are sugary or contain caffeine, or other substances that may affect your mood. Coffee might be good when you are tired, but it can be fuel for a panic attack when your anxiety is high.

Behaviorally:

◆ While you are getting ready, practice a few key things you can talk about. It will help you feel more confident while you are at the party.

◆ Find a place at the party where you can take a break for a few minutes if you get overwhelmed.

Develop your own list of what you need to shine:

Physically:

◆ _____

◆ _____

Behaviorally:

◆ _____

◆ _____

GOING TO PARTIES EXERCISE: COPING 101

Time: 5 to 10 minutes

You overcome your problems or challenges by coping. It is important to have a coping plan before walking into an anxiety-provoking situation.

When I am really stressed or I know I am entering a situation that will spike my level of anxiety, I reach into my coping toolbox.

- I listen to comedy because laughing fills my brain with endorphins (which help with pain tolerance) and dopamine (the happiness chemical).

- I problem-solve about what will trigger me, so I feel like I have more control and things won't catch me off guard as much.

- Mindfulness and relaxation are great go-to sources of support.

- The downward arrow technique (page 40) is great because I am not a brain surgeon, and my decisions do not affect anyone's mortality. Following the arrow to the worst-case scenario is helpful for me to see the relative insignificance of a situation.

With this in mind, let's create a coping plan.

My coping plan:

I will . . .

- _____

- _____

- _____

- _____

Dating

Being vulnerable is hard for all of us. Dating jump-starts vulnerability regardless of whether the dinner is free or not. Asking someone out is putting yourself out there in a way like no other. Going on a first date is exciting and anxiety provoking like an interview. *Woohoo! They said yes and we are going out. Oh no, now what?* The second and third date may increase anxiety from the pressure of affection or the need to make sure conversation keeps pace. *Should I say something or are they still talking?*

An awesome bonus of dating someone with anxiety like yourself is that the person with anxiety frequently has a higher level of emotional intelligence. This means that you are in tune with your emotions, which brings out awareness and self-reflection. If you can add to these qualities being able to clearly communicate your needs, healthy dating is around the corner.

The following exercises are intended to challenge your insecurities. You will develop an awareness of what is needed to survive your insecurities when feeling vulnerable by creating a counternarrative and by growing your confidence with communicating.

DATING EXERCISE: WHAT I NEED TO HEAR

Time: 10 to 15 minutes

In this exercise, you are going to identify your negative behaviors and assess whether these behaviors form a pattern. You will list the insecurities you feel when you think of dating. Then, you will write a counternarrative to your insecurity and give yourself a new narrative.

Common negative behaviors that most of us experience when we feel insecure include:

- ◆ Unhealthy thoughts

- ◆ Inability to focus

- ◆ Criticizing yourself or others

- ◆ Passive aggression

- ◆ Avoidance

- ◆ Perfectionism

What negative behavior happens when you feel insecure? Write next to each behavior whether it is a pattern.

Example:

NEGATIVE BEHAVIOR	PATTERN? (YES OR NO)
Critical of myself	Yes

Now write the insecurities that get in your way. Then, write the opposite of that insecurity to give yourself a new narrative.

INSECURITY LIST AN INSECURITY YOU HAVE ABOUT YOURSELF AND DATING	COUNTERNARRATIVE WRITE A COUNTERNARRATIVE TO YOUR INSECURITY
I stutter when I am nervous.	Everyone stutters sometimes. I am not the only person who gets nervous and my date will be just as nervous.

Reflection: Give yourself permission to sometimes feel insecure, as insecurity is normal. The goal is to face the fear and your lack of confidence with a healthy perspective. Additionally, we want to break the negative behaviors that may impact you and your relationships going forward.

DATING EXERCISE: PUTTING YOURSELF OUT THERE

Time: 10 minutes

When possible, asking someone out in person is best. You look brave and it is great practice for what is hopefully yet to come. You can see someone's body language, their sense of humor, and, with any luck, a smile. We usually communicate through texting or social media unless the person is standing in front of us, and even then we may still use technology to communicate, depending on who is around. Determining the best communication method is up to you.

Here are a few things to keep in mind when asking someone out:

◆ Be yourself: You are awesomely you and that is perfectly imperfect.

◆ Commonality: Find something you both like: movies, books, music, food, etc.

◆ Low risk: Invite them to something casual like coffee or lunch, not your cousin's wedding.

◆ Stay brave: If they say yes, awesome. If they say no, let it go. You do not want to go out with someone who is not interested: There are almost eight billion people on this planet.

Imagine the following messages on your preferred messaging app.

Thursday's Conversation:

Hey, what's your favorite restaurant downtown?

I like the pizza place on 2nd.

I like that place, too. You want to get lunch this weekend and walk around?

I am not sure about my schedule.

OK.

I have to check something and I will let you know.

I am around Saturday for most of the day.

OK, cool.

10 minutes later . . .

I can go to lunch Saturday but I have to be back by 4:00 P.M.

OK. 1:00 P.M?

Sure.

You want to meet there, or I can pick you up.

I will meet you there. I have stuff in the morning.

Ok. I will see you there.

See you.

Saturday's conversation:

I am on my way, see you soon.

See you soon. I am running a few minutes behind. Sorry.

Reflection: Putting yourself out there can be scary. If the conversation doesn't go your way, you still went up to bat! Rejection can feel awful and can suck in the moment. Here are a few key things to remember: There are a ton of reasons why someone says no. Do not personalize it, and do not generalize it, either. Stay out of the box when these thoughts start, and stay positive.

DATING EXERCISE: PACE AND RHYTHM

Time: 10 minutes

When communicating on a date, you want to develop a pace and a rhythm so the date does not feel like an interrogation or an interview. Creating a flow of communication will hopefully lower your anxiety and keep your inner critic quiet so those insecurities will not be your focus.

Here is a simple formula:

Talk + Listen → Collaborate = Burstiness Moments

First, you want to talk. Then, listen to what the other person is thinking. This should lead you to want to add to the conversation, which is the collaboration. Thus, you create simple burstiness moments.

Let's practice. Imagine you are at a café. You are sitting, talking about your classes and which teachers or professors you like over whatever drink you usually order.

> **YOU:** *My calculus teacher is so intense. She goes over things quickly and you cannot be sleepy in that class. The hardest thing is that the tests are all or nothing, so you have to be on point.*

Your date listens as you talk, then adds their contribution.

> **DATE:** *My teacher is really nice and goes over things a few times. No one in that class asks questions—it is such a quiet class. I think it's just me struggling.*

> **YOU:** *I am sure you are not the only one struggling, that class is just hard.*

Together you have a burstiness moment because you can both relate.

Find common ground in the conversation so that the flow does not seem forced. Then, your anxiety will not be the one leading the date. You will be.

Takeaways

Mark Zuckerberg said, *"The biggest risk is not taking any risk."*

- You learned how to build calm at home. Family relationships need navigation, just like most relationships.

- You learned guidelines for awkward conversations and brave rules that apply to most conversations in life. Remember to stay brave.

- Social media can impact your mental wellness. You now have a higher level of social media mindfulness to balance the demands of being available all the time.

- You learned tools to ask friends over, hang out, and go to parties.

- Dating can magnify your insecurities, but you have the power to create a counternarrative to keep them at bay.

CHAPTER 4

SCHOOL LIFE

In this chapter, you will learn how certain aspects of school such as social scenes, personal image, school activities, cliques, and awkward conversations may adversely impact you. Anxiety in these moments has the power to prevent us from accomplishing daily activities. You will learn simple strategies to manage those anxiety-triggered moments by breaking them into small pieces.

Mila began a new school this year due to a change in her family dynamic. She missed her friends, soccer, and her old life. Mila's anxiety was triggered throughout the day as she struggled with finding her classes and wandered around campus during her breaks and lunch. She listened to the expectations of her teachers as they reviewed the syllabi and began to feel overwhelmed about the academic demands of each class. Mila felt her anxiety building toward a panic attack and realized she had not managed her triggers. Mila began to use the strategies outlined in this chapter to reduce her symptomology.

Social Scene at School

Navigating through the varying paths of a school environment can be overwhelming and lead to social anxiety. When we do not have psychological safety, or the feeling that we will not be judged, it is hard to be ourselves. According to the US Census Bureau, there are more than 76 million students enrolled in school and college in the United States, which means you are not alone. Realizing that 76 million other students likely experience the same type of anxiety triggers is a way for you to center yourself. Your feelings in these situations have the power to trigger destructive or unhelpful thoughts; I call this the "rabbit hole." It is when one negative thought leads to another negative thought, which leads to another negative thought, and eventually you can get yourself in a deep, dark place that fosters self-loathing and lowers your self-worth. These thoughts make you feel "small."

Let's look at Mila's thoughts upon walking into one of her classes:

Everyone is looking at me. Where should I sit? I am going to pick the wrong seat. I am not going to have any friends. I hate this school already.

Mila began to go down the rabbit-hole spiral with her unhelpful and potentially destructive thoughts. Mila's questions became dark and eventually distorted. When this happens, our decision-making skills suffer. Let's look at some strategies to support Mila and examine how we can incorporate them into our lives to keep ourselves from following that rabbit into the very deep, dark hole.

SOCIAL SCENE AT SCHOOL EXERCISE: STOP THINKING

Time: 5 to 10 minutes

Stop Thinking is a way to train your brain to effectively prevent your negative thoughts from driving over you. Think of a cartoon in which the character has a little devil on one shoulder and an angel on the other. Can you picture it in your head? Now picture yourself with a negative you on your left shoulder and a positive you on your right shoulder. Sadly, that negative voice can overpower the positive voice in your head, tearing you down and making you feel small. With practice, you can learn to train your brain to tune out that irritating negative voice and redirect it to the positive voice. Think of the positive voice as the one who tells you your hair looks good in the morning, or that you are going to be unstoppable today. You have the power to silence negativity and choose to focus on the positive, which helps your brain feel good and supports constructive problem solving.

By stopping the thought pathway, your negative thoughts exit the thought freeway. Slowly, you can redirect yourself. With practice of "stopping" these thoughts, you will build a habit of not listening to that negative voice. Ultimately, your brain will stop generating the negative thoughts. Goal!

SOCIAL SCENE AT SCHOOL EXERCISE: TAKE YOUR THOUGHTS TO COURT

Time: 5 to 10 minutes

This is a cognitive behavioral activity that helps restructure your thoughts. Often, we have destructive thoughts that are very unhelpful and even distorted. Distorted thoughts are not logical, are irrational, and distort our perceptions of reality. We learned about distorted thoughts in chapter 2. They hinder our decision-making skills and can impact our relationships. When we take our thoughts to court, we must find evidence that makes each thought a true statement.

Let's look at one of Mila's distorted thoughts and take it to court:

Thought: *I am not going to have any friends.*

(Bonus points if you can name this type of distortion; there can be more than one answer.)

Evidence: What evidence can Mila use to prove this thought to be true or untrue?

◆ Did Mila have friends at her last school?

◆ Was she involved in clubs or sports before?

◆ Did Mila volunteer in her community?

Court is in session!

THOUGHT	EVIDENCE
I am not going to have any friends.	Mila played soccer at her old school. She had teammates to hang out with. Mila missed her friends from the move, so she had friends before.

We can reflect on Mila's past to demonstrate that this thought is irrational. At her last school, Mila played soccer and had a team around to support her. She can problem-solve by reflecting on what actions she took in the past to make her successful. As an example, Mila's first step may be to find out who coaches soccer at the new school. Once she meets the coach, the coach may introduce her to other players who can show her around campus. Then, just like at her last school, she may have a group of friends.

Practice on one of your own thoughts:

Court is in session!

THOUGHT	EVIDENCE

You can use this strategy in several situations. Get your gavel out and put on your lawyer face and figure out which thoughts belong in your brain. Hint: It's the helpful ones.

SOCIAL SCENE AT SCHOOL EXERCISE: CENTER YOURSELF

Time: 10 minutes

Social scenes foster anxiety for all of us at some point, like when attending a party, walking into an unfamiliar place, meeting someone new, and so on. If anyone says they have never felt social anxiety in these situations, they are telling tall tales! Our anxiety can take our quirks and idiosyncrasies and place them under a large magnifying glass that makes us feel self-conscious and insecure. Insecurity can be the most debilitating facet of our lives, especially as we are transforming into the people we aspire to be. When I feel my stomach tighten or sense racing thoughts infiltrating my brain, I take a step back and center myself. This is a mindfulness exercise that helps my brain stay present and my thoughts go not much farther than the room. When our thoughts take over, being present can become so difficult that you can sometimes feel like you are having an out-of-body experience! This is when you are just standing there and your brain feels detached and your actions seem a bit difficult to steer. But you can take the room back and center yourself.

Center yourself by focusing on the here and now. Tell your thoughts to *STOP*. Practice your deep breathing twice. Use one affirmation or mantra that empowers you to take the room back. You have tools: Let's use them together to create a chain reaction of calm.

My Image

Studies show a correlation between social media and low self-esteem, likely due to unattainable expectations (reel life vs. real life). Our self-image is how we see ourselves physically, emotionally, and cognitively (our thoughts). Self-image is created from social culture, family, friends, and media. We thrive when we receive compliments and close ourselves off when there is silence. Our inner critics can take hold of us and echo our negative thoughts and feelings.

When we have negative images of ourselves, we hide, cringe, and lack motivation to overcome those challenges. In the United States, a little more than 2 percent of people suffer from body dysmorphic disorder. This is a body-image disorder where one becomes extremely obsessed with an imagined or slight defect in one's appearance. People who suffer practice repetitive behaviors to hide or improve their real or imagined flaws. Just like avoidance, this is a temporary solution and prolongs negative feelings. Behaviors may include checking a mirror, excessive grooming, and camouflaging through safety items or activities like hats, makeup, clothing, or excessive exercise.

On the flip side, having positive thoughts, emotions, and behaviors around self-image fuels us to be happier. We see problems as opportunities and can challenge ourselves to overcome them because we have an invisible shield. We can shield ourselves from the negative messaging or trolling comments we see or hear.

Our self-image is inherently tied to our self-confidence. If we have a positive self-image, we have a higher level of self-confidence. Building self-confidence is a lifelong process. It is something that we need to continue to feed, help grow, and evaluate at many different stages. Together, we are going to take two steps forward by letting go of the negative messages from the present and past and learning to not compare ourselves to others. Last, we will channel gratitude inward, which will help us appreciate ourselves and build strong blocks of personal admiration.

MY IMAGE EXERCISE: LET IT GO!

Time: 10 minutes

Step 1:

Warning: This exercise is technology-free and you will need real supplies. Get paper and a pen. Take two deep breaths and prepare yourself to spill words onto the paper in front of you. Set a timer for 5 minutes. Write down ALL of the negative messages you have been telling yourself. Write down all of the negative messages you have heard from society, culture family, peers, etc., at ANY moment in your life. Every past negative thing you have heard, throw it up on this paper.

Step 2:

Remember, when things are hard, they are worth doing. These messages do not define you! Think of one positive thing that you believe about yourself: *I am unique, and no one is me.*

Step 3:

Take that piece of paper and rip it up into tiny pieces! Throw it away. Going forward, you will do this mentally. Throw those messages out, and do not listen. My go-to in these moments is to remember not to turn my head. Do not even give these negative messages an ounce of effort and they will dissipate into thin air.

Take a deep breath in and say the following out loud: "I am amazing and a beautiful work in progress who has no ceiling! I am aspiring to be my best self each day."

MY IMAGE EXERCISE: NO COMPARISON

Time: 10 minutes

Comparing ourselves to others is a sticky trap that we all walk into. Someone will always be wealthier, better looking, more fashionable, skinnier, smarter, etc.

The goal is to develop the best version of yourself that is also mentally well. You do this by setting healthy mental boundaries and expectations.

Here are a few key strategies:

1. Acknowledge that you are not perfect.
2. Have self-gratitude for all that you are.
3. Compliment yourself daily with an affirmation. Confidence should not be dependent upon others; it needs to come from within.
4. Quiet the noise. If social media, TV, magazines, and other media are bringing you down, do not look at them, unfollow them, or delete the applications altogether.
5. Self-forgiveness is gold. Forgive yourself and you will be able to forgive others.

Keeping these five strategies in mind, identify the things in your life that provoke you to compare yourself to others. Make a list of what provokes you on the left side of the chart. On the right side, write an action you can do to sidestep that trap.

COMPARISON	ACTION TO NOT GET TRAPPED

MY IMAGE EXERCISE: SELF-GRATITUDE

Time: 5 to 10 minutes

Self-gratitude relates to self-care and love. We rarely ever think of thanking ourselves, partly because it seems a bit awkward. The practice of self-gratitude contributes to a more positive attitude toward yourself and higher levels of self-esteem. One way for you to practice self-gratitude is to complete this workbook. Not only are you building calm in your life, you are building a stronger you!

Each day, when you get ready to go to bed, thank yourself for one instance where you made yourself grow, contributed positively to the world, challenged yourself, etc. You can do this in a journal, write it on a Post-it, say it out loud, or however you prefer.

Write one thing that you were grateful for today:

Make this a habit and part of your daily routine so that each day you add one brick of gratitude, thereby creating a solid foundation.

Classroom Presentations and Public Speaking

The National Institute of Mental Health reports that fear of public speaking affects approximately 73 percent of the population. This "glossophobia" has a variety of symptoms, such as increased blood pressure, trembling, muscle tension, nausea, panic, anxiety, and sweating. The freeze, fight, or flight response kicks in because the body senses an attack. Anxiety tricks us into thinking there is risk or danger ahead as if we are about to be eaten by a bear. Unfortunately, the fear of public speaking can impact your livelihood and future. Individuals with this fear may not get promoted to management positions and may earn 10 percent less in wages. Additionally, research indicates that public speaking anxiety can negatively impact college graduation rates by as much as 15 percent.

When you are nervous about delivering a classroom presentation or speaking in public, you are in good company. Keep in mind that most of the audience is experiencing similar feelings and emotions. In fact, three out of four people have the same fear. This also helps us empathize when someone is speaking in front of us. Give them a pass when they have a brain freeze or they stumble over a word. No one will remember in five minutes, anyway.

Presentations and public speaking are two things that are part of life during education and in the workforce. Together, let's rehearse strategies that will allow you to take control and feel confident when you deliver your next speech. We will be working backward, using a camera and learning to value ourselves. I want you to envision a mic-drop moment for yourself. Read on and let's get started!

CLASSROOM PRESENTATIONS AND PUBLIC SPEAKING
EXERCISE: WORK BACKWARD

Time: 10 minutes

Picture the end of your presentation. Close your eyes and imagine you are finished and your teacher, professor, or boss is blown away by what you just delivered. Picturing the ending will help guide your creativity and allow you to anticipate what the audience will ask. If you were sitting in the audience and listening to your topic, what would you want to ask or know more about? Think of the questions that the audience may have. Write those questions down.

If you are struggling to come up with questions, you can always do a small focus group with friends or family members: "Hey, I am making a presentation about jobs and what students need to be learning in school. What do you want to know about that? What do you think would be interesting to learn about?"

Questions:

1. _____

2. _____

3. _____

4. _____

Now let's build the presentation backward using these questions. One reason to do this is that you know your peers are usually the audience members. By predicting their questions, you will lower your anxiety about what they may ask. Also, it will add to your content and help you meet your audience where they are.

Take question 1 and see where you can insert that information in the presentation. Continue with questions 2 through 4. Once your presentation is complete, you can use the next exercise for practice. You may even create a new set of questions to add.

CLASSROOM PRESENTATIONS AND PUBLIC SPEAKING
EXERCISE: SMILE, YOU'RE ON CAMERA

Time: 10 minutes

Recording yourself using a smartphone or tablet is a great way to prepare for delivering a speech, giving a presentation, or reading out loud. If this seems too overwhelming, use the voice memo feature on your smartphone. When we record ourselves, we are creating an imaginal exposure and using in vivo exposure at the same time—a double strategy. This provides the opportunity to view ourselves from a different perspective. In fact, there are several benefits:

◆ Creativity: You must imagine your audience and their reactions. You also need to predict questions that may be asked.

◆ Expression: Watching your own face is a wonderful learning opportunity. You want to make sure that your expression represents your topic and the mood of your presentation.

◆ Confidence: Being in front of a camera will add a layer of anxiety that may mimic a real audience, thereby lifting your confidence for when the audience actually shows up.

◆ Boosted learning: Your learning capacity on this exercise is infinite. You will push yourself and develop a new method of learning using this exercise.

After you record yourself, there is one rule: **DO NOT JUDGE YOURSELF**. Be open to the things that went well, and open to the idea of improving areas that need development.

Write down one thing you did well:

_____

_____

Write down two things you need to develop or work at improving:

_____

_____

Write down another thing you did well:

_____

_____

This is called "sandwiching": one positive aspect, areas for improvement, and another positive aspect. This is a great approach when giving feedback to others or receiving feedback yourself, as it allows you to start and end with positivity.

Last step: Rerecord and celebrate the improvements!

CLASSROOM PRESENTATIONS AND PUBLIC SPEAKING
EXERCISE: VALUE YOURSELF

Time: 10 minutes

Every day, Amber dreaded going to class. Her teacher would randomly call on students for answers and explanations or to read out loud. Amber walked into class and stared at the ground, trying to avoid eye contact with the teacher. Throughout class, she struggled to pay attention to what was being discussed as she worried her teacher would call on her at any moment. When students were asked to read out loud, Amber would try to figure out which section was hers. Was the teacher going in order down a row or table? She feared stuttering and not knowing how to pronounce a word. She worried that the students around her would laugh and talk about her after class. Amber used the bathroom every class just to avoid not being called on for those five minutes. Amber's anxiety in class each day was preventing her from learning.

Today, Amber realizes she needs to make a change. She wants to talk to her teacher about her anxiety and how it is triggered when she is called on to read or for an answer that she was not prepared for.

We are going to help Amber start this hard conversation with her teacher. Imagine yourself walking into class before it starts. Take three deep breaths to feel relaxed. Remember to use the mindfulness exercises in chapter 2. Stay brave, with our five brave rules. Practice the following dialogue in a front of a mirror by reading the statement out loud.

> "Ms./Mr. [insert one of your teachers' names here], I wanted to talk to you about something; I hope this is a good time. I struggle to manage my anxiety in this class. It is hard for me when I am called on to read out loud or answer a question."

Reread the statement again. Practicing out loud is a great way to feel more comfortable.

Your statement:

Write a statement to someone you would like to tell about your anxiety triggers.

_____

_____

_____

_____

_____

_____

_____

_____

_____

SETTING BOUNDARIES

Setting boundaries is essential to mental wellness. Setting boundaries can be particularly difficult as it may make you feel uncomfortable. Particularly when you have social anxiety, maintaining boundaries may be a challenge. There are speed limits in driving; those boundaries keep us safe. Personal boundaries are the limits that keep us mentally, cognitively, and physically safe. One way to think of boundaries is with a cost-benefit ratio. The cost: You must inform people of where the line is. The benefit: You have clear communication and limits about what you are comfortable with emotionally, cognitively, and physically.

Having clear boundaries can spark hard conversations. You may need to assert yourself and show people the line, which can be uncomfortable and not fun. *See, this is my line. You cannot cross it; it is a boundary.* I joke that you'd better not call me before 6:00 a.m. unless you need a ride to the hospital. It is a simple boundary and an easy one to keep. Other boundaries are harder to keep, such as having a bedtime or not watching television after a certain time; they are more challenging because there is temptation. In relationships, lines can get blurred when boundaries are broken. We may feel fear of letting someone down or not pleasing them if we enforce certain boundaries.

When creating boundaries, sometimes an interpersonal conflict occurs. Your internal dialogue can cause you to second-guess yourself and question the cost-benefit ratio. People who are assertive or loud can steamroll us if we let our boundary lines waver. It is important to remember why you need that boundary: How is it keeping you safe? I need you to not call me before 6:00 a.m. because I am sleeping. Good sleep keeps me from being a monster in the morning! Think of an aggressive friend who borrows something but never returns it. They push you to borrow something else and insist as they tell you all the reasons they need to borrow it. You know you are letting them down by holding your boundary. Yet relationships are stronger with accountability. Boundaries help us develop our relationships in a healthy manner and keep them healthy. Know your value. You are worth the effort of maintaining a healthy line.

Dealing with Cliques

As humans, we yearn for group acceptance, affection, and guidance. Previously, we needed group acceptance for survival; we hunted and gathered in groups. Groups, cliques, and circles have benefits in the modern world. In fact, we do most things in groups, like working, learning, relaxing, worshiping, and playing. Avoiding groups and not belonging to them has detrimental effects, such as loneliness and poor self-esteem. Cliques provide us with resources and collective group support that a single friendship cannot provide.

Social anxiety may increase the threat of feeling rejected or shunned by the group. Often, even asserting yourself in a group causes anxiety to spike. Group dynamics may be intimidating. The most casual interaction may feel like an exhausting encounter. You may freeze and not know what to say, or you might hide in the background and not shine. One problem is that isolation leads to loneliness. Additionally, there are fewer resources for us if we do not participate or seek a clique. A group provides us with resources, information, and the sense of belonging we need to be more successful.

How do we lessen the pressure when dealing with groups and not succumb to escape and avoidance behaviors? Our self-talk has the power for good and evil. Positive self-talk supports our self-esteem and self-worth. Also, we control how small we allow other people to make us feel. Last, human connection is infinitely beneficial.

DEALING WITH CLIQUES EXERCISE: SELF-TALK

Time: 10 minutes

The pressure of fitting in and wanting to be liked is real for all of us. You may notice that you talk yourself out of something or talk down to yourself in these moments. You may begin to second-guess your value and what you contribute to the group. Your distorted thoughts can feel real. You start mentally filtering the messages and listening to them tear you down, one negative comment after another. You may need to complete a reality check, especially if you start to notice your self-talk becoming your "I can't" voice.

Think of marathon runners: 26.2 miles is a long way to go. Here are some examples of self-talk for a runner:

I can finish strong!

I trained for this moment.

I am powerful.

I am relaxed and focused with each step I take.

Now make your own self-talk list below. Get that inner cheerleader out!

_____

_____

_____

_____

_____

DEALING WITH CLIQUES EXERCISE: FEELING SMALL

Time: 10 minutes

When cliques feel intimidating, we tend to shrink. Our anxieties shout louder and louder and slowly we begin to fade into the background like a fly on the wall. Observing social situations is part of interacting in a social setting. We see the room, the layout, and the groups of people clustered together. We scan for friendly faces: Where and when we can insert ourselves into the conversation? What happens when we do not know anyone, or our friends are late? Do we join in and chat with strangers? Do we hide or pace around?

Consider the following:

Sophia walked into class and the teacher assigned a group project. The teacher instructed the students to organize into groups of four. Sophia did not know anyone in the class, so choosing group members seemed like a gamble. Sophia saw three students standing together, missing a fourth. One student in the group had never acknowledged Sophia—they walked by her every day and never gave a smile or a nod. As a few minutes ticked by, Sophia realized she needed to join a group before the teacher offered her up for adoption. Sophia could hear the teacher in her head: "*Which group needs a fourth member? Sophia does not have a group.*" Sophia knew she was a few moments away from her inner dialogue becoming a reality. She took a deep breath and told herself that awkward is what it is—awkward. She walked forward with butterflies in her stomach.

> **SOPHIA:** Hi, I do not really know people in this class. Do you need a fourth group member?

> **STUDENT 1:** I think we do.

> **STUDENT 2:** Yes, I guess we do.

> **STUDENT 3:** I hope you can write and you're not a flake.

> **SOPHIA:** I am a decent writer, and I don't flake.

They all laughed awkwardly and smiled.

Honesty is always the best policy with yourself and others. Sophia let them know she did not know anyone, so her cards were on the table. Be aware of your personal forecast and level of anxiety. Sophia acknowledged her anxiety and used a strategy to manage it. Repeat an affirmation that promotes your self-esteem and prevents it from taking a nosedive.

DEALING WITH CLIQUES EXERCISE: HUMAN NETWORK

Time: 10 to 15 minutes

A personal network is a group of caring, dedicated people who are committed to maintaining a relationship with a person in order to support a given set of activities. Having a strong personal network requires being connected to a network of resources for mutual development and growth.

No, I am not talking about a thousand friends on social media; I am talking about someone you would call to take you to the airport or pick you up if your car broke down.

Who is in your network?

Home: These are the people who live in your house or are family members that you can turn to. (Mother, father, siblings, aunt, uncle, grandma, etc.)

School/Work: Colleagues or people on campus whom you can call when you have a question, need help understanding something, or need help with a task. (Professor or teacher, counselor, student support personnel, etc.)

Community: These are people with whom you interact and whom you can lean on for help. (Friends, coach, neighbor, church members, etc.)

Make a chart of your human network. Some areas of your life may have a larger or smaller human network; this is normal.

HOME	SCHOOL	COMMUNITY

Reflection: How do these networks support you in your life?

_____

_____

_____

Awkward Conversations

Being authentic requires us to challenge ourselves to be honest and vulnerable. (I hope you are seeing a theme as we near the close of chapter 4.) Socially, we can feel like hiding in the corner or just giving in and melting into nothing. When silence hits, take a deep breath and collect yourself. Physically, when anxiety sounds the alarm, and your stomach tightens or butterflies float around, lean in. Awkwardness is a lifetime marathon, so let's start training!

Three types of awkward conversations that can be replicated in most of our lives between snacks are apologizing, advocating, and conflict resolution. All three require us to muster up self-confidence and trust ourselves that the challenge is worth the effort.

AWKWARD CONVERSATIONS EXERCISE: SORRY

Time: 10 minutes

Apologizing makes us feel vulnerable. It takes strength, humility, and transparency. Delivering an apology can be awkward and easily foster anxiety. We all make mistakes. In the beginning of this workbook in chapter 1, you outlined your core values. Review the three that you identified as your personal compass. They will guide you to stay true to yourself as we embark upon being more humble, transparent, and strong. Research shows that participants who affirmed their core values before apologizing had a higher level of self-image and were less defensive of their wrongdoing.

An apology has three key parts:

1. It fully accepts responsibility for the wrongdoing.
2. It is important to not attempt to justify why you acted a certain way or said a certain thing. You own the action and impact 100 percent.
3. Be sincere and offer to make things right. Ask, "What action needs to happen for me to not make the same mistake in the future?"

> "Amy, I am sorry I did not help you on that project. It was not nice of me to blow you off and I really wanted to help. How can I make it up to you? What else could I help you with now?"

Notice that there was no explanation justifying the behavior or wrongdoing.

When we apologize and take responsibility, it will add to our self-esteem and self-image. Remember to use your personal compass as guide to be your best version of you; keep affirming your perfectly imperfect self. Each day you grow and learn, and apologizing is part of that process.

AWKWARD CONVERSATIONS EXERCISE: ADVOCATE

Time: 10 minutes

"Advocacy: to change 'what is' to be 'what should be.'" —Anonymous

Advocacy is a critical life skill that can impact our academic, emotional, physical, and mental wellness. Advocacy is how we stand up for ourselves, ask questions, seek help, and challenge the status quo. In this exercise, Ryan received a lower grade on an assignment than he feels he earned. Ryan is going to have an awkward conversation with his teacher.

> **RYAN:** Ms. Brown, I would like to talk to you about my grade when you have a few minutes. When would be a good time to talk?

> **MS. BROWN:** Ryan, grades are determined by how students complete their work. Please see the rubric for further clarification.

> **RYAN:** Ms. Brown, I understand that. I have read the rubric and I have a few questions. Do you think later today may be good, or should I come back tomorrow?

> **MS. BROWN:** Today is fine. Come back at 2:00 p.m., please. That is when I am available.

> **RYAN:** Thank you, Ms. Brown. I will be back at 2:00 p.m.

2:00 p.m. arrives and Ryan approaches Ms. Brown

RYAN: Ms. Brown, I read the rubric. On section one I was marked down several points. I am not understanding what I missed.

MS. BROWN: Ryan, you did not explain your answer and provide examples. I gave you half credit because you listed the items but did not provide the explanation or examples.

RYAN: Ms. Brown, the rubric says to identify. It does not say that I need to explain or provide examples. [Ryan shows the rubric.] When I think of identify, I think list. That is what I did, I listed.

MS. BROWN: Well, I think my expectation to explain and give examples was not made clear. I will give you the full points. Thank you for bringing this to my attention. I appreciate how you asked to speak with me as well.

RYAN: Thank you for your time, Ms. Brown.

Advocating for yourself with grades or clarifying expectations helps you, students in the future, and the instructor. As awkward as it may be, advocating is a true life skill. Side note: Never be rude, disrespectful, or self-righteous. When I make a mistake, I like for someone to point it out with grace.

Write how you would advocate for a grade change. Remember to stay brave with the brave rules from chapter 3 (page 51).

AWKWARD CONVERSATIONS EXERCISE: MIDDLE GROUND

Time: 10 minutes

Group projects, teams, and collaboration impact our lives at school and work. When confrontation shows up in these dynamics, we may tend to run and hide. There are four conflict resolution styles. These are represented in the following table.

CONFLICT TABLE

	I Win	I Lose
You Win	Win-Win	Lose-Win
You Lose	Win-Lose	Lose-Lose

Win-Win: Both sides win. We each feel that we are walking away with what we wanted. This is where we bargain, negotiate, and compromise to come together.

Lose-Win: I lose, and you win. I must give up something in the situation and you walk away benefiting from my loss. Often, this can create tension in a relationship, such as feeling resentment, holding a grudge, and feeling low self-esteem. Or we are so nice that we forget to value ourselves.

Win-Lose: I win, and you lose. I am leaving the conflict or disagreement winning. However, I may have lost the relationship because I am willing to sacrifice it for the win. Think of a time in an argument where you wanted to just beat the other person, instead of hearing them out. I always think of this situation as being self-righteousness versus the right thing.

Lose-Lose: We both lose. We both leave hurt, and there is no solution. Think of a time where you and another person said mean things to each other that neither of you meant. You both said them in anger (or hurt) to cause harm to the other person. This can happen when our personal forecast is storming and so is the person in front of us. It is like two tornados colliding. The result is that two towns are destroyed.

The best result can come when we focus on the goal and seek agreement. I try to understand where the other person is coming from and explain my needs so that I may also support their needs. We hear what the other person wants, and we can articulate what we want. Finding the middle ground may take time. Value yourself equally in the conflict and be careful not to sacrifice the relationship. Win-win is the goal!

Takeaways

"Daring to set boundaries is about having the courage to love ourselves even when we risk disappointing others." —*Brené Brown*

- We learned you are one of 76 million students in the United States.

- You learned how to train your brain using Stop Thinking.

- We can now Let Go of negative messages and make sure the cheap-seat opinions stay where they belong: in the very back row.

- We learned strategies to overcome glossophobia.

- Setting boundaries is what can keep us mentally well and our relationships healthy.

- The word "cliques" may be annoying. Their benefits are worth the effort and investment! They provide our lives with the resources, information, and social support that positively impact our lives. Stronger together!

- As awkward conversations come about, remember to apologize, advocate, and find the middle.

CHAPTER 5

EVERYDAY LIFE

Public encounters and making small talk impact our social lives daily. Struggling to order at a restaurant, the fear of eating in front of people, and making forced quick decisions can all hold us back from beneficial social contact. These fears interrupt our relationships and our human need for positive connection.

Nicholas felt isolated from meaningful relationships even though he was surrounded by people. His anxiety closed him off from others, and loneliness edged closer and closer. Simple tasks were big hurdles for Nicholas. He dreaded most public transactions, from checking out at the grocery store to ordering food at a restaurant. He felt that no one would understand if he told them that he felt abnormal. His friends were so effortlessly social; he admired their snap decision skills and quick responses. Nicholas wanted to talk to people with ease and knew his anxiety prevented him from succeeding. There was a moment when he realized he wanted something different for himself. Nicholas built his awareness and used the strategies in this chapter to foster deeper, more meaningful daily interactions.

How Do I Feel Outside of Home and School?

Loneliness is becoming an epidemic. Research shows it is hitting Generation Z (those born between the mid-1990s and early 2000s) the hardest, and Millennials (those born from 1981 to 1996) are the second loneliest. Cigna Corporation and Ipsos, a market research firm, conducted a large-scale survey of 20,000 adults in the United States, and they discovered that rates of loneliness had doubled from a decade ago. The study had important findings:

+ One in four felt that there are people who understand them.

+ Approximately half of the participants sometimes or always felt alone.

+ Slightly more than half felt they had meaningful in-person social interactions daily.

Nicholas realized he was different from his friends, and he wanted to develop skills so his social hurdles would be lower. His avoidance behaviors were preventing him from fully engaging. Part of his awareness was learning to understand his behaviors and how they protected him from his fears.

Fear can hold us back from success, adventure, and being the best versions of ourselves. We can get in our own way, as fear may be the only voice we listen to; we give it more reverence than it has earned. Very rarely do we frequent dark alleyways or put ourselves in situations where we can be mauled by a bear. Yet we know what fear feels and sounds like and how it holds us back. The following strategies are designed to empower you to not let anxiety be your first definition, so you can build quality relationships and minimize the effects of loneliness.

HOW DO I FEEL OUTSIDE OF HOME AND SCHOOL EXERCISE:
QUALITY OVER QUANTITY

Time: 10 minutes

You can be the one everyone knows while being the one no one knows. Having a high quantity of relationships has been shown to leave us feeling lonely. Research indicates that the quality of our relationships is more important than how many relationships we have in our lives. Additionally, research shows that we want to be positively viewed in our relationships. When we feel this, we are more willing to invest, and our interactions are more genuine. Let's look at some guiding attributes that help define quality relationships:

- ◆ **Empathy:** We want someone who can understand us without judgment, who can put themselves in our shoes, and who will stay when things are hard and celebrate the wins.

- ◆ **Trust:** We need to feel that we can share things and they will not be let out into the world. We need people in our lives who are honest and can also hold us accountable.

- ◆ **Respect:** Mutual respect is key, where we both admire the other's individuality. We need to feel that we are valued in our relationships; that we are treated appropriately without malice, manipulation, or games.

- ◆ **Transparency:** This is where we feel we can be our real selves. We can do and say the things we feel without judgment. We do not have to put on a show; we can just be ourselves.

- ◆ **Cheerleader:** We need people to support us in order to be the best versions of ourselves, and to challenge us to reach our goals. They cheer us on, and we equally invest in them.

In chapter 4, you mapped out your human network. Look at the previous attributes and feel free to add to the list. What do you need for a high-quality relationship?

Write your attributes below:

_____

_____

_____

_____

_____

_____

HOW I FEEL OUTSIDE OF HOME AND SCHOOL EXERCISE:
GET OUT OF YOUR OWN WAY

Time: 10 minutes

When fear begins to hijack your life, remind yourself that you have full control of your vessel. You have heard the negative propaganda fear has been telling you, and the time to stop listening is now. Taking a risk is scary. You may need to remind yourself that 76 million students do scary things every day.

Let's reflect on a few questions that you can answer in this workbook or by using a journal, technology, or a sheet of paper.

How do you hold yourself back?

_____

_____

What message(s) do you need to silence?

_____

_____

What do you need in order to stay engaged when fear begins to creep closer?

_____

_____

Write three ways you can keep calm and get out of your own way when fear begins to take hold.

_____

_____

_____

HOW I FEEL OUTSIDE OF HOME AND SCHOOL EXERCISE:
CHANGE THE NARRATIVE

Time: 10 minutes

Think of a road. There are smooth parts, potholes, twists, and turns. Our lives are like roads. We can have an identified destination but many routes to get us there. Everyone has a story of how they came to be the person they are today. We may have defined ourselves by anxiety or certain stories. *I am the girl with glasses who hides in the corner hoping no one notices. I am the guy who is part of the background waiting for his moment.* We try to fortune-tell what others think about us and may even act accordingly. You are your own author, however, and your story is continuing this journey.

Draw your road. Outline the moments that were important to you, the potholes you tripped on, the turns you took, and the twists that defined you.

- What is the narrative you have been telling yourself thus far?

- How do you want to change it going forward?

- Whom do you need help from in your life for these changes to be successful?

- When it is difficult, what will be your personal affirmation to motivate you?

Store Cashiers, Pizza Delivery, and Other Transactions

Adulting. Adulting is where we as individuals execute tasks that are necessary to be successful in life. If we are truly being honest, these duties or tasks are not a fun time. They include grocery shopping, errands, making doctor appointments, paying bills, physically going into a bank, making phone calls, ordering things over the phone like pizza delivery, getting gas—all the things we need to do to live successfully. When performing these adulting tasks on the phone, I find it painful sometimes. How long will I be on hold, or how many times do I need to repeat the command to get what I need? *Customer service, Billing, Operator, Cancel service.* The waiting can be anxiety provoking with the mere anticipation of the exchange. My least favorite part is when they ask my name; 99 percent of the time my name becomes "Ally." I am pretty sure I said "with an 'S,'" but at this point I second-guess my ability to say my own name. Now I will spell my name first just to avoid being called Ally. I empathize with anyone who has a more uncommon name than mine. I suggest spelling it or adopting a go-to phone personality name like Michelle or John.

Part of adulting is using our small-talk skills to complete said tasks and engaging in those environments with others. Typically, these interactions are a few minutes of awkwardness. If there is awkwardness, I have great news for you: You can handle doing most things you do not like for five minutes. I really don't like running, but I will run for five minutes.

Interacting with difficult customer service people can switch a sunny-day forecast to annoyed, to frustrated, to mad. If we flip it, when I have a lovely person who is helpful and treats me with respect and kindness, my forecast can have birds singing and a rainbow. Using our soft skills and being aware of our forecast ahead of time are two key factors. If I am already having a rough day, adulting may not be a great idea. However, avoidance can lead to late fees and consequences. Additionally, more experience engaging in these interactions will make you an expert. I know you can become an expert with a few skills for your toolbox. First, you need to make a list, prioritize, and plan. Second, know when you need help. Third, ask for the help you need.

STORE CASHIERS, PIZZA DELIVERY, AND OTHER TRANSACTIONS EXERCISE: ADULTING

Time: 10 minutes

Adulting takes making lists, prioritizing, and planning the tasks that need to be accomplished. These to-do lists are important because they keep us organized and accountable. An alternative is to brain dump all the tasks you need for the week. Your cognitive labor force is less likely to go on strike, and it will lessen the ruminating thoughts spinning in your brain. The second thing is to prioritize that list by due date or importance. Last, a goal is a wish without a plan. When you want things handled, plan. Brian Tracy, an author and motivational speaker, says, "Eat That frog." This means that you should do the most difficult thing on your to-do list FIRST. If you do the hardest thing first, the rest of the day is butter-smooth. Using this format will lower your anxiety and lessen the intrusive thoughts about all the adulting you need to accomplish.

Below is a sample chart you can use to begin when creating your own list, or, there are many apps for your phone and computer that can assist with this as well. You may need to test a few out and find one that works for you. More important, find one that you will use consistently.

TO-DO LIST	PRIORITY	PLAN

STORE CASHIERS, PIZZA DELIVERY, AND OTHER TRANSACTIONS EXERCISE: HELP? YES!

Time 10 minutes

Accepting help can feel awkward, especially with an overeager salesperson or employee. My knee-jerk reaction is, "Just looking, thank you." And then I turn and walk away. Avoidance, anyone? When you are interacting in a retail environment, remember that you have the power to say "yes" just as much as "no, thank you." Receiving help can make us feel vulnerable, like we are giving up control over what we obtain. Often we even tell ourselves we are imposing. You may need to remind yourself that the person who is offering help is paid to work there. This may lessen the burden of asking for help. Another setback may be that you do not feel worthy of receiving the help.

STORE CASHIERS, PIZZA DELIVERY, AND OTHER TRANSACTIONS EXERCISE: PERMISSION SLIP/GIFT CERTIFICATE

Time: 5 minutes

Strong, smart, efficient, amazing, talented, successful, and [insert any complimentary adjective here] people are all of those things because they asked for help. I am sure you have heard the phrase "It takes a village." Well, it can be a village, or you can substitute with your own version of the word that is more *you*: my circle, my people, my community, my family, my network—whatever you want to name it. Here is the thing: Our perception of asking for help may be skewed. Remember the distorted thinking way back in chapter 2: Sometimes we tell ourselves narratives that are not accurate, like "Asking for help makes me weak." Shenanigans! When you ask for help, you show strength! Strength that you know how to leverage resources, strength in your relationships, and strength in yourself. You are worth helping! When you are adulting at a store and you need help, advocate for yourself and say, "Excuse me, could you please help me find . . . "

I am going to give you a priceless gift. It is a permission slip and gift certificate all in one. It will give you permission, and it is also a gift to you so that you may aspire to be the best version of yourself. It never expires, you can use it infinitely, and it's good for the rest of your life. Please take a photo of it and save it to your favorites as a reminder. You are priceless!

PERMISSION SLIP

I, _____ , give myself permission to ask for help when I need it. I will not shame myself or say self-deprecating statements when I need help.
I will celebrate my awareness and my amazing use of the resources in my life to be the best version of myself!

Love,

Me

ANXIETY AND FOOD

Anxiety can impact your relationship with food. It is well known that unhealthy eating patterns can cause mood swings. Blood sugar fluctuations and nutritional imbalances are often to blame. Without a steady source of fuel from the foods we eat, our minds and bodies are not functioning at their best. Research shows that stress and food have a significant connection. Food has become a source of coping for many people, which is why the majority of adults in the United States are overweight. The media often shows the cliché example of a girl who breaks up with her boyfriend and in the next scene is downing ice cream. She just opens her mouth, swallows, and shoves more in her face. (My daughter even asked me if this "really happens" to people.)

It is true there are connections between stress and food. We often like high-calorie, high-fat foods when we are stressed, like ice cream or french fries. The problem with emotional eating is that when we are stressed our brains do not recognize the full feeling, and we can overeat. On the opposite side of the spectrum, some people lose their appetites and forget to eat altogether.

Below are several self-reflection questions to promote awareness of your relationship with food and anxiety.

When your anxiety hits, do you eat more or less?

Do you justify a latte (or another favorite treat) because you are stressed?

When anxious, do you eat nothing, and then your mood sinks lower?

Do friends or family make comments about your eating habits?

Be mindful of how you use food for coping. If you cope using food, replace it with a healthier option like taking a walk, calling a friend, or completing one of the exercises in this workbook. It is important to have a healthy relationship with food, and awareness is the first step.

Going to the Movies

Going to the movies seems like it should be an anxiety-free activity. Unfortunately, the climate of violence has shaken our confidence at the movies. When you add that distant fear to an already heightened level of anxiety, it becomes complex emotionally. There are many interactions that occur in theaters that may leave us feeling socially awkward. The pressure to order tickets, choose the right seats, interact with the concession stand worker, pay for high-priced popcorn and snacks, find your seat in a dimly lit theater, and sit through movie previews—being self-conscious eating delicious movie snacks as you are aware of each loud bite of popcorn—may leave you feeling exhausted. Your social anxiety may kick in with these various tasks. The anticipation of the movie may also be uncomfortable as well, and it can feel like anxiety.

A movie theater may feel like a dark boxed room, making you feel trapped. Be aware of feeling claustrophobic or agoraphobic. What do you need in order to not let fear lead the charge in these moments? One recommendation is to go at a time when there are fewer people around. You may need to skip the opening weekend and make that a goal to work toward.

Anxiety can also show up when we have empathy for the characters in the movie. Empathy is where we share feelings and relate to another person. When you share feelings of shame or embarrassment, it can make you feel powerless and helpless. Watching a character embarrass themselves or feel shame can be difficult. You may cringe and find yourself relating to the character as if it were your life. It may remind you of a moment when you embarrassed yourself and trigger those feelings and anxiety. It is always hard to watch the other characters shame a character for their actions. These moments can stir up negative emotions, and our empathy may feel intense.

Going to the movies, though, is a part of social culture. Avoiding movies may negatively impact our relationships, and we may miss out on fun times. Movies are a great way to help us connect to each other, learn things, see new perspectives, and reflect on our own lives. When there is a positive message in a movie, I leave feeling warm and inspired, and I want to be that character in real life, shining for others and making positive changes in the world.

Mindfulness can be a great tool when we are feeling overwhelmed and exhausted from moviegoing. Centering yourself will allow you to regain control and focus on the moment without getting too far ahead of yourself with negative thoughts and feelings. In the following exercise, you will learn to connect with your body, practice mindful eating, and use touch to develop a sense of calm.

GOING TO THE MOVIES EXERCISE: BODY SCAN

Time: 5 to 10 minutes

A body scan is where we bring attention into our body; it is like a body check-in. There are three key components to a body scan:

- Pause to check in with your body

- Breathe to create awareness and attention

- Connect with each part of your body

The body scan process has us slow down and stay in the moment to connect with our bodies, bringing us a sense of calm. Try to keep a sense of openness about this process. Let's try it together: Follow these prompts and notice where you begin to feel a sense of calm.

First, take two deep breaths and clear your thoughts. Notice where your body is in relation to the moment. What time of day is it? Are you feeling tension in any area of your body? What is your personal forecast (anxious, upset, frustrated)? Notice what is happening without judgment and just let your body exist. Start from the top and notice your face and head, thinking of each section. Go to your neck and feel it connected to your back. Feel the chair against your body, how it touches your back, giving it a small hug. Take two deep breaths and follow that feeling from your back into your arms. Stretch out your fingers and hands, feeling each sensation. Take a deep breath and feel the air come in and out of your chest down to your stomach. Feel your stomach and back, into your legs, knees, and down your legs into your toes. Wiggle or stretch your toes and feel how they are separate and attached. Take two deep breaths and feel each section of your body connected to each other.

Hopefully you now feel a sense of calm. A body scan is a great mindfulness activity that you can do in a movie theater, a restaurant, a classroom, or really anywhere. It helps you connect to your body and the moment in time, helping you stay present.

GOING TO THE MOVIES EXERCISE: EATING MINDFULLY

Time: 5 minutes

You can do this exercise with any food; I find candy to be the easiest to start with. We will use chocolate as our example. Please get a piece of chocolate before you continue. The goal is to center all your attention on the actual food you are eating to become present. Read the following prompts and enhance your mindfulness toolbox. Be open, stay curious, and observe something new. If your thoughts start to wander, politely bring them back to focus without judging yourself.

CHOCOLATE:

Pick up your chocolate candy. Notice the packaging, the container, the wrapper. Observe the colors, shapes, and writing you may see. Feel the weight of the candy. Examine all the small details you may have overlooked before. Feel the packaging by touching the edges. Open the packaging. Watch your hand and fingers work together. Listen to the sounds as you open or unwrap the piece of chocolate. See if you can now smell the chocolate; bring it closer to your nose until you can. Does the smell remind you of anything or provoke a sensation in your body? Do you have thoughts about the chocolate? Is your mouth anticipating the chocolate? Are you thinking about a second piece of chocolate already? Slowly, take a small bite of the chocolate. Feel it in your mouth and feel it on your tongue. Be aware of when you want to swallow so you can have another bite. Swallow, and notice any sensations or feelings associated with the chocolate.

REFLECTION:

How was this different from how you usually eat chocolate? What did you notice that you did not pay attention to before? Think of your eating habits: How can you apply this mindfulness to other moments?

GOING TO THE MOVIES EXERCISE: SOOTHING TOUCH TO PERSONAL HUG

Time: 5 minutes

Numerous studies have shown that touch can have incredible benefits for our emotional and physical health. Touch helps us communicate, bond, and even physically grow when we are infants. Neuroscience has taught us that touch gives us feelings of compassion and reward by releasing oxytocin. Oxytocin is referred to as the cuddle hormone or love hormone because it combats cortisol, the stress hormone.

Our brains are wired to protect us from being eaten; when our nervous systems become overwhelmed, our brains produce cortisol. Physically, our hearts race, we sweat, we have shortness of breath, and we experience stomach pain or nausea. When oxytocin is produced, the amygdala sends a signal of calm, giving a sense of safety and control. Through touch, we can reduce anxiety symptoms. In this exercise you will learn a form of tapping, which will produce oxytocin.

1. Put your open hand on your chest so your thumb and index finger can feel your collarbones on each side.
2. Lift your hand up and down gently in a tapping motion.
3. Rub your hand clockwise in small circles, making sure you rub over the collarbone.

Doing this for several minutes sends your brain the same signal as a hug would. Essentially, this is our own personal hug. You may have naturally done this in moments of stress and not known why. Now you will know that a soothing touch going forward can mitigate stress.

Restaurants

Eating out is one of the most common social activities in our culture. As our busy lives run like the Energizer Bunny, we keep going, going, and going to eat out. Eating at restaurants and ordering complicated lattes and dressing on the side can seem easy for some, but painfully tedious for those who experience social anxiety. Research shows that 20 percent of people who have social anxiety fear eating in front of others.

Eating in front of others plus anxiety may manifest in "what-if" situations:

◆ What if I do not know what fork to use?

◆ What if my hands shake?

◆ What if I spill on myself?

◆ What if I eat too fast or too slowly?

- What if the food is spicy and my face turns red?

- What if I talk with my mouth full?

There is a series of tasks when going to a restaurant. First, we must decide what to order, which can be stressful on its own. A popular chain restaurant has more than 300 items on its menu; I always order the same three things to avoid decision fatigue. Decision fatigue is where we become exhausted from making decisions, and weighing our options becomes cloudy. Depending on the noise level of the restaurant, ordering can feel like a feat. If you feel like a thousand eyes are watching your every movement, eating and drinking can feel grueling. Anxiety may trigger us to eat too much, or to become parakeets and eat crumbs. To conclude, the check comes; this can be an extremely awkward moment unless you chatted about the bill ahead of time. Unless you ordered the lobster, just split the check so no feelings are hurt, and avoid the weirdness of doing the math.

How do we dodge these awkward anxiety-provoking mishaps and carry on? How do we not feel a thousand eyes on us when we are eating? We take one bite at a time. Make smart decisions you can embrace, and, last, stay grounded. Using these strategies will add to your toolbox and you can use them in most eating experiences, like parties, award dinners, and more.

RESTAURANTS EXERCISE: DECISIONS, DECISIONS . . .

Time: 10 minutes

Decisions can deplete our energy and squander valuable brain power. Research shows we toggle between making 300 decisions a day—no wonder decision fatigue is real. As mentioned previously, the "what-if" game is not fun to play and can drain us from using our brain power to solve bigger problems, like world hunger. One strategy is to set a time limit for yourself for decisions. It will lessen your cognitive labor, thereby lessening expenditure of your energy on one decision.

Seating.
Sit where you will feel comfortable. This is the first decision that you need to make to feel more secure.

Ordering.

The power of habit can reduce our decision fatigue. Think of the things you usually like to order at a restaurant. Does this place have something similar? Asking for help is usually my go-to. The people who work at the restaurant are the experts. What are their recommendations?

Eating.

It is important that you evaluate your pace. When we are feeling anxious, we tend to eat quickly or painfully slowly. Two results can occur: your stomach hurts, or you just move the food around like the plate is a dance floor. If you are worried that people are going to stare at you eating, focus on one bite at a time. Save your mental energy for choosing dessert.

Check, please.

Forty-four percent of Americans identified that money is their number one stress. If you know that the check is awkward and stressful for you, chat about the check ahead of time. Spending your energy on how the check will be split may drive your brain in circles. Checks are being paid at one million restaurants every day, and yours will get paid, too.

Think back to the past: Which decisions at a restaurant drained you? Write them out.

_____

_____

_____

_____

_____

_____

Awareness is the first step. Now, to make those decisions feel less burdensome, can you use the 3-minute decision timer? The previous guidelines are also great suggestions for saving your cognitive labor resources.

RESTAURANTS EXERCISE: ONE BITE AT A TIME

Time: 10 minutes

When the "what-if" questions start peppering your brain, slow them down, one bite at a time. Here are a few things that will support lower anxiety while eating.

1. Do not order things that are messy and will add stress. If you are worrying about how to eat the food, you will exhaust your energy quickly. Order something you feel confident about.
2. Focus on eating one small bite at a time. You do not have to eat all your food; you just need to eat some of your food. Start eating that elephant one bite at a time!
3. Use your napkin as a safety blanket. Make sure your napkin is in your lap to protect you from spills and sauce on your face. If you get a little sauce on your face you will have it handy to wipe your mouth.
4. If you are going to a restaurant with courses, meaning lots of silverware, read Emily Post. She was an American author and socialite, famous for her knowledge and writing about etiquette. Knowing which fork to use will give you confidence. You will have one less thing to worry about. (Eat on the left, bread plate, drink on the right, inside, outside silverware, and dessert silverware is at the top because it's the best.)

RESTAURANTS EXERCISE: 5 SENSES GROUNDED

Time: 10 minutes

Restaurants are a great place to use all of your senses: sight, touch, sound, smell, and taste. You can use them to get grounded. Being grounded is where you establish a sense of inner calm by being aware of yourself and your surroundings. This is a great exercise you can take with you to a party or most other places. You can make it a fun game. There are numerous ways to do the five senses of grounding. This exercise counts down from five to one, the goal being to help you reregulate and take control of your senses, which will help you feel present. If your anxiety is still at its peak, play it again and challenge yourself to secure your center.

Sight: Find five things that you can see.

◆ Look for things that are the same color; you can pick your favorite color.

◆ Seek and find things that have a commonality (things that go together, like kitchen items or school supplies).

Touch: Find four things you can touch.

◆ If you are sitting, touch the chair, bench, or stool. Feel your back or bottom and evaluate how comfortable it is. If you are standing, feel the floor under you. Is it carpet or hardwood?

◆ Touch something that is soft, like a pillow, a napkin, or a tablecloth.

Sound: Find three things you can hear in the room.

◆ Listen to people talking.

◆ Can you hear things outside, like traffic, birds, or the door closing?

Smell: Find two things you can smell.

◆ Restaurants have powerful food smells.

◆ Can you smell any perfume or cologne around you? Or your own?

Taste: Taste one thing that you can recognize.

◆ You can drink your water or beverage, or taste bread or your food.

◆ What do you have access to within reach?

Small Talk in Public Spaces

When we are in public, like waiting in line at a store, in a waiting room, on an airplane, or on a train, confined spaces tend to generate small talk from strangers. I know we have all been taught about stranger danger, and that you may dislike enforced small talk. Escape and avoidance are not an option, since the person standing in line with you wants to be your new friend for the next five minutes. Interactions such as these are often unavoidable and are part of our days. Social anxiety can impact how we feel after the adoption of our spontaneous friend. We may feel self-conscious, nervous, and emotionally drained by our reactions. How do we change this narrative for ourselves?

Let's cognitively restructure how we feel about small talk. If you view small talk as a pointless level of interaction that sucks up time and space in your day, it will be painful. Now I want you to take all the negative thoughts you have about small talk and counteract them with a simple statement: *Small talk challenges me to learn something new and practice mindfulness.* Social situations can teach you something about yourself or others most of the time. Small talk can help you learn to connect to others with low stakes—meaning, you do not have to go out of your way and take your five-minute best friend to the airport. Also, small talk is a minor investment in our day; if someone is willing to invest in me, I take it as a compliment. Practicing quick conversations in line or in a waiting room can lower your anxiety when the stakes are higher in the future. Embracing your new friend for five minutes is a simple opportunity to grow a true soft skill.

Small talk helps us interact successfully and congenially with others by using our personal characteristics. It can help our mindfulness grow through listening, strengthening our soft skills, and creating a light touch. As with most things, small talk can be fun and enjoyable with the right perspective!

SMALL TALK IN PUBLIC SPACES EXERCISE: FROM BLAH, BLAH TO MINDFUL

Time: 5 to 10 minutes

Small talk can be ordinary, and often we dislike its forced nature. Our choice to not engage in small talk is unfeasible in many situations. One positive note is that we can use small talk as a great mindfulness activity. Mindfulness can help us stretch ourselves by focusing us on the present moment.

Goal: Silence the all-pervading to-do lists in your head or the unhelpful thoughts invading your brain. Stay present and in tune by engaging with your new five-minute friend.

Here are some guiding questions and points to help you:

◆ Notice your surroundings and others around you. What do you notice that you did not see before?

- Become aware of the person's personal forecast. Are they having a good day, or they are needing to connect with someone such as yourself?

- Focus on their tone of speech and the words they use. Did you hear a new word?

- Observe their body language and be mindful of your own.

- When breathing, feel your chest go up and down as you listen to the person.

- Keep your intention to stay engaged and mindful.

Mindfulness in these moments will help us lessen the focus on our own anxiety and focus on the person in front of us. It is hard to listen to others when our anxiety is triggered. Small-talk mindfulness will train our brains to listen and stay present in the relationships in which we want to make deeper investments.

SMALL TALK IN PUBLIC SPACES EXERCISE: SOFT SKILLS

Time: 10 minutes

Small talk is a soft skill. Soft skills help us interact by allowing us to communicate successfully and congenially with others using our personal characteristics. They help us read others, so we can understand emotions and insights. Soft skills take time to acquire. They are not taught in a classroom; rather, they are learned through our interactions with others. We need soft skills to help us navigate in school, the workplace, networking, and our own social lives.

Noah is sitting in a waiting room for his appointment. He is bored and feels annoyed that he has been waiting so long. Another person walks in and sits next to Noah and initiates a small-talk conversation.

STRANGER: Hey, I like your shirt.

NOAH: Oh, thank you.

STRANGER: Have you been waiting long? It always takes a long time here.

NOAH: Yes, I have. I wish they would hurry up—sitting makes me tired.

STRANGER: Me too—I hate sitting for a long time.

NOAH: Do you want a magazine? They have a bunch here.

STRANGER: Um, no thanks. It weirds me out how many people have touched those magazines.

NOAH: Dang, I never thought of that. Gross.

STRANGER: One time, I was waiting and a lady rubbed the sample perfume on herself. I almost threw up.

NOAH: [laughs] Who does that?

STRANGER: I know, right?

NOAH: Oh, it's my turn now. Have a good day.

STRANGER: You, too.

....

Reflection: The stranger was able to read that Noah was a bit lethargic. They connected with Noah by asking about the wait time, something they both had in common. The stranger told a quick funny story that made Noah laugh. Noah perked up, and engaging with his new five-minute friend made waiting a little less painful. Soft skill, acquired!

SMALL TALK IN PUBLIC SPACES EXERCISE: LIGHT TOUCH

Time: 10 minutes

One of the most powerful skills I have ever learned is a light touch. It is a way for us to use small talk to engage others, so they feel seen. A light touch is a small connection that you make through paying attention, reading someone's emotions, knowing their intentions, and acknowledging them verbally. When someone notices a small thing in my life and makes a comment, I always feel like I matter. All people matter, right? Let's acknowledge them. Think about when someone comments on something new, like when you get a haircut or new clothes. It makes us feel like someone is paying attention and that they see us doing our thing (haircut, dance move, presentation, taking a trip, etc.). These light touches can foster bigger connections, and, sometimes without noticing, we build resources within our personal networks.

Example: When I frequent a business and I see the same people who work there, I always try to learn their names and introduce myself. It is surface-level, quick small talk and is low-stakes. "Hey, I am Sally. _____, it's nice to meet you. I will see you next time. Have a great day." I can grow my soft skills and make genuine connections. Also, introducing yourself is a lifelong occurrence; practice never hurts and can only be helpful.

Using small talk as a light touch sidelines anxiety. It takes the focus off you as you focus on someone else. The intrusive thoughts of what you are going to do and say can take a vacation.

Takeaways

- Loneliness and phobias allow fear to narrow our choices, leaving us feeling isolated.

- Food and stress can be friends for life. We need to develop a healthy relationship with food and coping.

- Empathy helps us forge connections to others by sharing feelings. It can sometimes be painfully uncomfortable and remind us of our own fears.

- With one million restaurants in the United States, we can tackle our anxiety by eating an elephant one bite at a time.

- Small talk leads to light touches, which can alleviate anxiety and help build resources within our personal networks.

CHAPTER 6

LOOKING AHEAD

If you take one thing away from this workbook, I want it to be this: *Anxiety doesn't disappear. Embracing its varying levels will challenge you throughout your life.* Through the tools you have acquired, you are more equipped to manage the flare-ups, the triggers, and daily stress!

This chapter will help you identify your challenges, bring awareness and clarity about what works for you, establish a prevention plan, and last, make a support plan going forward. As we rally to the end, I encourage you to be conscious of avoidance. Finish strong, go the distance, and continue to push yourself to the finish line!

Targeting Your Biggest Challenges

Fear is our biggest challenge in life. It holds us back from starting things, it keeps us stuck in one place, and it can prevent us from being ourselves. We determine how it defines the path in front of us. Let's show fear who has the real power: you! Your future is paved by the way you walk: with a purpose and a plan. We all have challenges, and planning for them makes the struggle a little less burdensome.

First, we need to reassess where your social anxiety impacts your life. This will help with reflection and your process. Next, look at what worked for you and what did not. Your plan needs to be individualized in order to arm your brain with strategic, sustainable tools that work on the anxiety challenges that are uniquely and awesomely yours.

POST-TEST

Time: 10 minutes

In this table are the same 10 frequency statements from chapter 1. You will have an opportunity to look back at chapter 1 for your answers; hold that thought for now, please. Previously, our goal was to assess how social anxiety may be impacting your life. We are going to shift the focus and use this as an opportunity for reflection. The goal of this activity is not to judge yourself; rather, it is to reveal your personal growth and areas for further development. When answering, listen to your instincts; stay brave and transparent to yourself. Answer the questions, using data from the last week.

QUESTIONS IN THE LAST WEEK . . .	ALWAYS	OFTEN	SOMETIMES	RARELY	NEVER
I imagine how people are judging me in social situations and I fear I will embarrass or humiliate myself because of what I might say or do.	☐	☐	☐	☐	☐
I have feelings of discomfort in most social situations.	☐	☐	☐	☐	☐

QUESTIONS IN THE LAST WEEK . . .	ALWAYS	OFTEN	SOMETIMES	RARELY	NEVER
I worry about what I am going to say days before an activity (party, project, social situation).	☐	☐	☐	☐	☐
My daily interactions in my life (home, school, community, and relationships) are affected by my anxiety.	☐	☐	☐	☐	☐
I am tremendously aware of my actions and fear offending someone or being rejected.	☐	☐	☐	☐	☐
I prefer to be in the background in a group situation and not the center of attention.	☐	☐	☐	☐	☐
I avoid social situations and use technology as much as possible, so I do not have to interact with people.	☐	☐	☐	☐	☐
I am self-conscious that I will blush, sweat, or have a trembling voice when in social situations.	☐	☐	☐	☐	☐
Thinking about social situations stresses me out and surviving them can be exhausting.	☐	☐	☐	☐	☐
I leave a social situation questioning my actions and obsessing over the things I said or what my physical actions were.	☐	☐	☐	☐	☐

Now look back at the answers in chapter 1. Compare to this post-test. Were there areas of improvement? Did your level of anxiety lessen its intensity in some areas?

I am happy with my improvement. Congratulations on working hard to move your answers to the right. Remember, this is a continual process, and maintaining mental hygiene is a daily task.

My answers were not what I hoped for. Change takes time. If your results were not what you wanted, do not stress—mental wellness is a process for all of us. Continue to work hard and keep investing in yourself; you are worth the time and effort!

REVIEW

Time: 10 to 20 minutes

Self-improvement can be thought-provoking, challenging, and worth every minute of investment. Let's put your ninja reflection and awareness skills to the test. Flip back through the book and note areas that you have highlighted, underlined, or made notes pertaining to which skills were most useful on this workbook journey.

Now take your highlighted or underlined list and make a top five (or ten) list.

COMMITMENT TO MYSELF

Time: 10 minutes

Make the commitment that fear, and the anticipation of fear, will not lead you forward. To overcome your biggest challenges, you must make a commitment to yourself. We intrinsically feel happier from the act of giving; it connects us to our personal network and society. We need that same level of compassion and commitment for ourselves. Below is a contract, with yourself. Without shame, guilt, or blame, make the commitment that you will not give up on yourself.

I, _____, commit to making my mental wellness a priority in my life going forward. I will consistently work to be the best version of my imperfectly perfect self from today forward. I am a work in progress, who is working on progress.

_____   _____
Signature   Date

The goal now is quality over quantity; it is about your starred top five or ten list. Think of using these top exercises as your individualized mental wellness plan. How can you commit to overcoming your challenges using these five or ten? What can you consistently commit to for yourself that will become a habit for your mental wellness? Reflect below:

_____

_____

_____

_____

_____

_____

_____

_____

_____

_____

Finding What Works for You

You have been working hard to challenge your thoughts and identify your feelings and triggers. You have taken assessments and learned more about anxiety than you thought you would ever know. You have established your core values and made your mental wellness a priority. Optimistically, this work should have created a new perspective for you about your social anxiety. You have put the hard work in, and we need to make sure that hard work is sustained through a maintenance plan that works for you.

Living mentally well requires mental hygiene through which we intentionally work to maintain our wellness. Just as we floss and brush our teeth every day, we need to employ regular maintenance strategies to keep our brains healthy. You need to first build an action plan in order to successfully implement your new perspective. An action plan makes a goal tangible by putting "legs" on an idea. The legs are the steps you need to take to make the idea a reality. Second, establishing an accountability partner will support your idea and keep you accountable to your goal. Last, reflection will help you reestablish your goal when you waver off the path. It provides you the opportunity to course-correct and keep going.

GOAL SETTING EXERCISE: NEW PERSPECTIVE, ACTION PLAN

Time: 10 minutes

Anxiety does not own you; it is a part of you and a part of every human on earth. Here you will reflect on your personal forecast history—the moments that shook you or caused a wave to ripple through your life. We will use your history as a point of reflection to prevent recurrences. From those moments you will develop an individualized plan that is 100 percent your own. Last, you will put the legs on the plan. Your action plan will be a reference guide to the past and a goal for the future.

Step 1. Create a personal forecast history. When did your anxiety flare up? Where did the stress fault lines show up in your life? List three to five areas, activities, or moments when your anxiety was not managed.

_____

_____

_____

_____

_____

Step 2. List your top five exercises for your individualized plan.

_____

_____

_____

_____

_____

Step 3. Develop a sustainable action plan. Your action plan should be detailed enough to outline what you need to reach your goal. Think of what steps you need to take to be successful. Below is a sample action plan with an example for reference. Feel free to get creative and make it yours!

PERSONAL FORECAST HISTORY: ANXIETY NOT MANAGED	INDIVIDUALIZED PLAN EXERCISES	ACTION PLAN
When I want to ask a question in class or when I need help academically.	Soothing Touch to Personal Hug	When I feel anxious and want to ask a question, I can rub or tap my collarbone to center myself.

GOAL SETTING EXERCISE: ACCOUNTABILITY PARTNER

Time: 10 minutes

Setting goals feels amazing; accomplishing them feels like magic. Get ready to partner up! Research shows we need human connection because it drives us to better ourselves. Establishing an accountability partner will help you maintain responsibility, lower the number of excuses you are allowed to use, help create ownership, and support your personal empowerment expedition. They will keep you on track; when you waver or fall, they help you dust off your knees. Having an outside perspective provides insight when it is hard to see what is in front of us and when we cannot see what is holding us back.

Who should be your accountability partner? Great question! A great accountability partner has the ability to give you feedback you can hear. For the feedback loop to be beneficial, you must be willing to listen and sometimes hear hard things. This requires a real sense of psychological safety, where you can show vulnerability and let someone in. Additionally, they will prevent you from self-deprecating and saying negative things about yourself to yourself. An accountability partner will let you vent, and then ask, "Now, what are you going to do about it?" This person does not let you act like a victim. They are your cheerleader through and through.

Establish who in your life will hold you accountable, cheer you on, and not let fear hold you back. My accountability partner will be _____
_____.

GOAL SETTING EXERCISE: REFLECT → COURSE CORRECT

Time: 10 minutes

Self-refection is an amazing tool and can act like an accountability partner, holding you responsible for achieving your goals. With this level of self-reflection, success is on the horizon. As mentioned before, our lives have twists and turns and potholes we stumble over. When you get off track, get feedback, reflect, and course-correct. Shaming or verbally assaulting yourself is not cognitively efficient, nor is it going to make you feel better. Put that energy toward making magic happen.

Let's take the following example: You want to ask a question, either in class or because you want to request academic help. You tell your accountability partner that you avoided asking for help and now you are struggling. Your accountability partner will help you plan a course correction for tomorrow.

YOU: I didn't ask what the teacher meant and now I am not sure if what I am doing is what they want.

PARTNER: That sounds frustrating.

YOU: I really want to be able to ask a question in class without overthinking it.

PARTNER: What's your plan to not overthink it?

YOU: I need to figure that out.

PARTNER: You know you get nervous and shut down, right? What if you wrote the question down and then asked it with the paper?

YOU: That's not a bad idea. Is that weird?

PARTNER: Getting help is not weird, and you will ask the exact question you need. How else? What is another way you can ask for help?

YOU: I can email them that I want to ask a question before class. Then, I have to show up, right?

PARTNER: That is true. You will have to ask, or it would be rude. You can do this, and it will get easier each time.

Your accountability partner stayed with you in the moment without judgment. They did not let you hide in the corner or give in to defeat. They were empowering and challenged you to think of a second solution with support.

Relapse Prevention

Life happens! We can have the best intentions to live a flawless life—"happily ever after," right? Reality looks a bit different; life is courageous and messy. Being human is having compassion for ourselves and others. When we stumble, we need to take compassion along with us on the fall. We need to stand up, dust off our knees, and take a step forward. The intention to prevent relapse should be an infinite goal, and we need to add a pinch of grace room.

The first step in prevention is awareness and acceptance. We all have some level of social anxiety, and when it shows up, we need to be aware and accept that the path is a bit rougher to navigate. Part of the awareness is looking at your schedule. For most of us, our lives are overscheduled and the white space in our day or week is miniscule amounts of downtime. We need to plan to recharge when our batteries are running low. The consequences of a low battery are sickness, tension headaches, feeling exhausted, and being reactionary in our behaviors. This is when we regret something we said and have to apologize. Instead of running yourself emotionally ragged, plan recharge activities throughout the day. When the relapse happens, you will have a few tools ready to fix the leak.

RELAPSE PREVENTION EXERCISE: ACCEPTANCE OF ME

Time: 10 minutes

Anxiety + Me = Me. Acceptance is a process where we welcome or consent to something; we embrace something without resistance. Self-acceptance can seem like an odd concept. We need to welcome and embrace ourselves without judgment. This is not an easy task, and it is complicated by the messaging we receive from media and society and the messages we narrate for ourselves. How do we fully embrace ourselves? It is a magical question. We all are working on embracing ourselves to some degree. The answers are unlimited, and they probably change at different stages of our lives. It is a question we should be asking ourselves regularly. We all need ammunition when we waver and feel insecure or unsure of ourselves. As our anxiety does not define us, and is only a part of us, we are just ourselves.

Anxiety + Me = Me.

Step 1. Set a timer for 3 minutes. Brainstorm everything that makes you *you*; how anxiety is a part of you and not the full definition of you.

Step 2. Using your brainstorm activity, write how anxiety has taught you something about yourself you did not know.

Step 3. Write one thing about yourself that you need to remember when your thoughts become judgmental and unaccepting.

Use this exercise to express how you embrace acceptance of yourself. Refer to it when negative messages attack your brain. Remember the formula Anxiety + Me = Me: anxiety plus me still equals me. You are still the perfectly imperfect you.

RELAPSE PREVENTION EXERCISE: OVERSCHEDULED

Time: 10 minutes

You may not even realize you are feeling overscheduled. Coaches, professors, parents, community leaders—they all want a 100-percent commitment. How does that math add up? It does not; it is bad math. It is impossible to give 100 percent in everything you do. We give 75 percent because 100 percent every day, all day, is make-believe (unless you are an Olympian, and then you probably do give 100 percent).

Here are some symptoms of feeling overscheduled:

◆ You are tired and lethargic.

◆ You have physical symptoms, like stomachaches, headaches, physical pain, etc.

◆ Your sleep is disturbed; you are not sleeping well and are having bad dreams or night terrors.

◆ You are no longer interested in things that you used to enjoy, like movies or ice cream.

- Your grades are dropping.

- Your mood has flown south for the winter.

- You avoid family and friends.

- Your best friend is missing in action.

One way to evaluate is to use a physical paper planner. I know this is a bit retro and is one more thing to carry around. Using technology to calendar and schedule is helpful. Research shows, though, that these reminders and dings cause us to become reactive, not proactive. If our schedules are on paper, we tend to be more proactive. We can foresee when a tornado is about to hit! I have included a weekly planner you can copy. I use my paper planner and my technology together. Technology provides the now for me: today, in this moment. The paper planner provides the horizon of my week. I am able to see the full week and find the white space I can use to do nothing or plan a recharge activity.

SUN	MON	TUE	WED	THU	FRI	SAT	NOTES AND TO-DO LIST

Gratitude for the week:	Priorities:

RELAPSE PREVENTION EXERCISE: RECHARGE!

Time: 10 minutes

Even the Energizer Bunny needs a recharge. We need to ensure that we have moments in the day, week, month, and year where we intentionally recharge. Recharging activities should match the level of your depleted battery pack.

- ◆ A quick recharge can be something as simple as reflecting on all the things you accomplished for the day.

- ◆ Or, when you feel anxiety beginning to tighten the muscles in your body, take the hint and take a quick stretch break.

- ◆ Another great strategy is to connect with someone and let them know you need a recharge (I hope you just heard a small voice saying "accountability partner").

Make a list of five quick things that you can do throughout the day when you need to recharge your battery pack:

1. _____

2. _____

3. _____

4. _____

5. _____

Finding Support

As you continue on your path forward, I encourage you to keep seeking support. Why? Because successful people ask for help! I encourage you to consider therapy. We all need a safe place where we can lean in, obtain skills, build awareness, and have protected time to simply invest in a better self. That investment will help you course-correct to be the best version of yourself.

The tricky part is finding a therapist you connect with. Not all therapists are as funny as I am (wink, wink). Sometimes you need to therapy-shop. I recommend seeing someone a few times before you stop seeing them. Especially during your first experience of going to therapy, expectations about what you think therapy looks and feels like can provoke anxiety.

Therapy Options

Before considering seeking out a provider, there are a number of therapy options to consider. Let's take a look at some possibilities.

Teletherapy uses technology with a webcam, microphone, and speaker system, and therapy is provided over the internet. The benefits are the flexibility and access for rural or remote areas. It is a different therapeutic relationship than in person, and it is important to be mindful of what you need.

Individual therapy is where you work with a therapist one-on-one. This is a safe, confidential space where you have the opportunity to explore feelings, thoughts, beliefs, and behaviors to improve aspects of your life. Sometimes you can have a family member come into the session for support.

Family therapy can be helpful for any family to learn how to cope, build stronger connections, and support each other in stressful times, such as during grief, financial changes, or family stress. It looks at the system of a family—what is working and what relationships or aspects can be strengthened.

Group therapy can be an empowering environment where people like you are working on a common challenge, from anxiety, to grief, to learning how to be an adult. Often, we feel isolated in our struggles, and group therapy normalizes them. We are not alone and can benefit from learning from and the support of others.

Access to Therapy

What if you don't have a friend or family member who can suggest a trusted therapist, or you aren't having any luck therapy-shopping on your own? Where else can you turn?

Insurance. If you have insurance, using the number on your insurance card or the company website can help guide you to services.

College/school. Often, schools have counselors, student support services, a school social worker, or a mental health and wellness center on campus that can link you to services on campus or in your community. Colleges usually have low-cost to no-cost support on campus. There are many options for services, and if you are feeling overwhelmed on how to access them, ask for help.

resources

For many of us, our primary resource for acquiring information is the internet. The internet is an incredible tool, but it can be its own dark and scary black hole. Proceed with caution when you are reading and scrolling. Remember that as humans we need each other; there is no substitute for meeting and connecting with someone in person.

APPLICATIONS

As the internet is evolving and changing, I will recommend a few key applications that are free on iOS or Android.

Self-Help for Anxiety Management (SAM)

SAM-App.org.uk

SAM is an anxiety toolkit that helps you track anxious thoughts, and can teach you self-help techniques such as calm breathing. SAM also has a helpful community forum for anyone in need of additional support.

iChill

ChillApp.com

When you are stressed or worried about someone, iChill can teach you the Community Resiliency Model, a set of self-help skills. You will learn how stress affects the mind and body and practice wellness skills.

MY3 App

MY3App.org

The MY3 app helps you to stay safe in a crisis as well as define your network. Through this app, you have the ability to be prepared when you have thoughts of suicide by reaching out to others. It helps you prepare a safety plan and identify coping strategies, distractions, and who you can call, and it lets you easily access the National Suicide Hotline as well as 911. I recommend this app for both prevention and education; inform a friend.

BOOKS

There are several books I highly recommend for mental health and wellness and to improve your life overall. These are the top five that I feel have benefited my life; they were recommended to me to help with self-improvement. To fit them into your busy lifestyle, try one or two as audiobooks!

How to Train a Wild Elephant: And Other Adventures in Mindfulness
by Jan Chozen Bays

The title is just the start. This book teaches mindfulness in the most efficient and tangible way, with simple practices that you can easily make a habit.

The Power of Habit: Why We Do What We Do in Life and Business
by Charles Duhigg

Habits are an amazing phenomenon. How we have created them and how they impact our lives is important to understand so we can make the changes we desire.

365 Days of Wonder: Mr. Browne's Precepts
by R. J. Palacio

Need inspiration? This is a quick, fun daily fix! It also reminds me to be kind to others and myself; the world needs more kindness.

Braving the Wilderness
by Brené Brown

I am a fan of all things by Brené Brown. Her candor and storytelling connect challenging concepts in small bites. She is transparent and uses research to make the world a better place by understanding and explaining human relationships.

references

CHAPTER 1

Alden, L. E., and P. Bieling. "Interpersonal Consequences of the Pursuit of Safety." 1998. *Behaviour Research and Therapy* 36 (1): 53–64. doi: 10.1016/s0005-7967(97)00072-7.

Bertolote, José. "The Roots of the Concept of Mental Health." 2008. *World Psychiatry* 7 (2):113–116. doi: 10.1002/j.2051-5545.2008.tb00172.x.

DoSomething.org. "11 Facts about Anxiety." https://www.dosomething.org/us /facts/11-facts-about-anxiety#fnref11.

Ford, Emily, with Michael R. Liebowitz and Linda Wasmer Andrews. *What You Must Think of Me.* 2007. New York: Oxford University Press.

Furukawa, T. A., J. Chen, N. Watanabe, Y. Nakano, T. Ietsugu, S. Ogawa, T. Funayama, and Y. Noda. "Videotaped Experiments to Drop Safety Behaviors and Self-Focused Attention . . ." 2009. *Journal of Behavior Therapy and Experimental Psychiatry* 40 (2): 202–210. doi: 10.1016/j .jbtep.2008.08.003.

Harris, Russ. "The Complete Set of Client Handouts and Worksheets from ACT Books." https://thehappinesstrap.com/upimages/Complete_Worksheets _2014.pdf.

Kim, E. J. "The Effect of the Decreased Safety Behaviors on Anxiety and Negative Thoughts in Social Phobics." 2005. *Journal of Anxiety Disorders* 19 (1): 69–86. doi: 10.1016/j.janxdis.2003.11.002.

Mayo Clinic. "Social Anxiety Disorder (Social Phobia)." Last modified August 29, 2017. https://www.mayoclinic.org/diseases-conditions/social-anxiety-disorder /symptoms-causes/syc-20353561.

Semel Institute for Neuroscience and Human Behavior. "How Do You Cope?" https://www.semel.ucla.edu/dual-diagnosis-program/News_and_Resources /How_Do_You_Cope.

Smith, Melinda, Jeanne Segal, and Jennifer Shubin. "Social Anxiety Disorder." Last modified November 2019. https://www.helpguide.org/articles/anxiety /social-anxiety-disorder.htm.

Social Anxiety Association. https://www.socialphobia.org.

SocialAnxiety.com. https://www.social-anxiety.com.

WebMD. "What Is Social Anxiety Disorder?" https://www.webmd.com/anxiety -panic/guide/mental-health-social-anxiety-disorder#.

CHAPTER 2

American Psychological Association. "What Is Exposure Therapy?" https://www .apa.org/ptsd-guideline/patients-and-families/exposure-therapy.

Burns, David D. *Feeling Good: The New Mood Therapy.* 1980. New York: William Morrow & Company.

Didonna, Fabrizio, ed. *Clinical Handbook of Mindfulness.* 2009. New York: Springer.

Lennon, Lori. "Can Meditation Make You a More Compassionate Person?" April 1, 2013. Northeastern University College of Science. https://cos .northeastern.edu/news/release-can-meditation-make-you-a-more -compassionate-person.

Neff, Kristin. "What Is Self-Compassion?" Self-Compassion.com. https://self -compassion.org/the-three-elements-of-self-compassion-2.

Self-Help.tools. "Interoceptive Exposure." https://www.albany.edu/counseling _center/docs/AAW/self%20help%20resource%20library/Interoceptive _Exposure.pdf.

Worldometer. https://www.worldometers.info/world-population.

Zessin, Ulli, Oliver Dickhäuser, and Sven Garbade. "The Relationship Between Self-Compassion and Well-Being: A Meta-Analysis." 2015. *Applied Psychology: Health and Well-Being* 7 (3). doi:10.1111/aphw.12051.

CHAPTER 3

Anderson, Monica, and Jingjing Jiang. "Teens, Social Media & Technology 2018." May 31, 2018. Pew Research Center. https://www.pewresearch.org /internet/2018/05/31/teens-social-media-technology-2018.

Arao, Brian, and Kristi Clemens. "From Safe Spaces to Brave Spaces." In Lisa M. Landreman, ed. *The Art of Effective Faciliation: Reflections from Social Justice Educators.* 2013. Sterling, VA: Stylus Publishing, 135–50.

Experiments with Google. "Digital Wellbeing Experiments." https://experiments .withgoogle.com/collection/digitalwellbeing.

Green, A., M. Cohen-Zion, A. Haim, and Y. Dagan. "Evening Light Exposure to Computer Screens Disrupts Human Sleep, Biological Rhythms, and Attention Abilities." 2017. *The Journal of Biological and Medical Rhythm Research* 34 (7) 855–65. doi: 10.1080/07420528.2017.1324878.

Guendelman, Simón, Sebastián Medeiros, and Hagen Rampes. "Mindfulness and Emotion Regulation: Insights from Neurobiological, Psychological, and Clinical Studies." 2017. *Frontiers in Psychology* 8: 220. doi: 10.3389/fpsyg.2017.00220.

Kiyonnathewriter. "Higher & Higher: 11 Athletes & Rappers Who Meditate." July 10, 2018. *The Urban Daily.* https://theurbandaily.com/playlist/higher -higher-11-athletes-rappers-who-meditate.

Koudenburg, Namkje, Tom Postmes, and Ernestine H. Gordijn. "Disrupting the Flow: How Brief Silences in Group Conversations Affect Social Needs." 2011. *Journal of Experimental Social Psychology* 47 (2): 512–15. doi: 10.1016/j.jesp.2010.12.006.

Netsanity. "Teens and the 'Constant Pressure' of Social Media." January 2, 2018. https://netsanity.net/teens-social-media.

Rutledge, Pamela. "The Pressures of Social Media: Should I Disconnect?" July 19, 2016. *Psychology Today blog.* https://www.psychologytoday.com/us/blog /positively-media/201607/the-pressures-social-media-should-i-disconnect.

Shafer, Leah. "Social Media and Teen Anxiety." December 15, 2017. Harvard Graduate School of Education. https://www.gse.harvard.edu/news/uk/17 /12/social-media-and-teen-anxiety.

Shafer, Leah. "The Ups and Downs of Social Media." May 16, 2018. Harvard Graduate School of Education. https://www.gse.harvard.edu/news/uk/18/05 /ups-and-downs-social-media.

Statista. "United States: Number of Social Network Users 2017-2023." https://www.statista.com/statistics/278409/number-of-social-network -users-in-the-united-states.

CHAPTER 4

Baker, J. R., and J. L Hudson. "Children with Social Phobia Have Lower Quality Friendships Than Children with Other Anxiety Disorders." 2015. *Anxiety, Stress, and Coping* 28 (5): 500–13. doi: 10.1080/10615806.2014.978863.

Forsyth, Donelson. "The Psychology of Groups." *Noba Textbook Series: Psychology.* https://nobaproject.com/modules/the-psychology-of-groups.

HEALTHbeat (blog). "Giving Thanks Can Make You Happier." Harvard Health Publishing. https://www.health.harvard.edu/healthbeat/giving-thanks-can -make-you-happier.

Ma, X, Z. Q. Yue, Z. Q. Gong, H. Zhang, N. Y. Duan, Y. T. Shi, G. X. Wei, and Y. F. Li. 2017. "The Effect of Diaphragmatic Breathing on Attention, Negative Affect and Stress in Healthy Adults." *Frontiers in Psychology* 6 (8): 874. doi: 10.3389/fpsyg.2017.00874.

Murphy, John. "New Epidemic Affects Nearly Half of American Adults." January 11, 2019. *MDLinx.* https://www.mdlinx.com/internal-medicine /article/3272.

Prokopets, Elena. "22 Things Only People with Social Anxiety Would Understand." *Lifehack.* https://www.lifehack.org/articles/communication/22-things-only -people-with-social-anxiety-would-understand.html.

Rodebaugh, T. L., M. H. Lim, K. C. Fernandez, J. K. Langer, J. S. Weisman, N. Tonge, C. A. Levinson, and E. A. Shumaker. "Self and Friend's Differing Views of Social Anxiety Disorder's Effects on Friendships." 2014. *Journal of Abnormal Psychology* 123 (4): 715–24. doi: 10.1037/abn0000015.

Schneier, Franklin. "Social Anxiety Disorder." http://www.columbia.edu/itc/hs
/medical/psychmed2/3_2005/Schneier-SocialAnxietyDisorderBW.pdf.

Schumann, Karina. "An Affirmed Self and a Better Apology: The Effect of
Self-Affirmation on Transgressors' Responses to Victims." 2014. *Journal of
Experimental Social Psychology* 54: 89–96. doi: 10.1016/j.jesp.2014.04.013.

Science of People. "How to Ask Someone Out: 8 Steps for a Yes Every Time."
https://www.scienceofpeople.com/how-to-ask-someone-out.

Telch, Michael J. "False Safety Behaviors: Their Role in Pathological Fear."
University of Texas Laboratory for the Study of Anxiety Disorders.
https://labs.la.utexas.edu/telch/files/2015/08/Safety-Behavior-Handout
-latest-8.1.15-1.pdf.

Witvliet, M., M. Brendgen, P. A. van Lier, H. M. Koot, and F. Vitaro. "Early
Adolescent Depressive Symptoms: Prediction from Clique Isolation,
Loneliness, and Perceived Social Acceptance." 2010. *Journal of Abnormal
Child Psychology* 38 (8): 1045–56. doi: 10.1007/s10802-010-9426-x.

CHAPTER 5

American Psychological Association. "Stress and Eating." https://www.apa.org
/news/press/releases/stress/2013/eating.

Cigna and Ipsos. "Research Puts Spotlight on the Impact of Loneliness in the
U.S. and Potential Root Causes." May 1, 2018 https://www.cigna.com
/newsroom/news-releases/2018/new-cigna-study-reveals-loneliness-at
-epidemic-levels-in-america.

Feinstein, David. "Acupoint Stimulation in Treating Psychological Disorders:
Evidence of Efficacy." 2012. *Review of General Psychology* 16 (4).
doi: 10.1037/a0028602.

Jackson, Terry. "7 Principles for Developing Quality Relationships."
December 27, 2016. *AboutLeaders.* https://aboutleaders.com/7-principles
-quality-relationships/#gs.tp2mpl.

Lambert, M. J., and D. E. Barley. "Research Summary on the Therapeutic
Relationship and Psychotherapy Outcome." 2001. *Psychotherapy: Theory,
Research, Practice, Training* 38 (4): 357–61. doi: 10.1037/0033-3204.38.4.357.

Levinson, C. A., and T. L. Rodebaugh. "Social Anxiety and Eating Disorder Comorbidity: The Role of Negative Social Evaluation Fears." 2012. *Eating Behaviors* 13 (1): 27–35. doi: 10.1016/j.eatbeh.2011.11.006.

Queen, T. L., R. S. Stawski, L. H. Ryan, and J. Smith. "Loneliness in a Day: Activity Engagement, Time Alone, and Experienced Emotions." 2014. *Psychology and Aging* 29 (2): 297–305. doi: 10.1037/a0036889.

index

about the author

Sally Annjanece Stevens, LCSW, M.Ed., PPSC, and her husband, Nathan, a chemistry teacher, devote their personal and professional selves to education, investing in beautiful diverse faces every day. Their two children, Kirin (son) and Finnley (daughter), challenge and inspire Sally personally and professionally, adding all the magic to life.

Sally uses humor and a pinch of New York City directness to destigmatize mental health. Establishing equity for all children has guided her to focus on prevention, psychoeducation, and advocacy. Sally has a gift for building relationships by being her genuine self through transparency about her mistakes and celebrating her wins with those who have helped her along the path. She began her career as a school social worker in various high schools in Los Angeles Unified School District, as she loves working with teenagers. Currently she is a school mental health administrator for LAUSD. Sally sits on the board of Friends of School Mental Health, a nonprofit that supports students in crises affecting their ability to attend and learn at school. Additionally, Sally is the founder of Anchor Yourself Wellness in Huntington Beach, which offers mental health services and consultation for children, individuals, and families.